STUDENT LEARNING IN HIGHER EDUCATION

NEW PATTERNS OF LEARNING SERIES
EDITED BY P.J. HILLS, UNIVERSITY OF LEICESTER

Student Learning in Higher Education

JOHN D. WILSON

A HALSTED PRESS BOOK

CROOM HELM LONDON

JOHN WILEY & SONS
New York — Toronto

© 1981 John D. Wilson
Croom Helm Ltd, 2-10 St John's Road, London SW11

Published in the U.S.A. and Canada
by Halsted Press, a Division of
John Wiley & Sons, Inc., New York

British Library Cataloguing in Publication Data
Wilson, John D.
    Student learning in higher education —
    (New patterns of learning series)
    1. Universities and colleges — Students
    2. Study and teaching
    I. Title   II. Series
    370.15'2   LB1027
    ISBN 0-7099-0238-7

Library of Congress Cataloging in Publication Data
Wilson, John D.
    Student learning in higher education.
    "A Halsted Press book."
    Bibliography: p.176.
    Includes index.
    1. College teaching — Handbooks, manuals, etc.
2. Learning, Psychology of — Handbooks, manuals, etc.
3. College students — Psychology — Handbooks, manuals, etc. I. Title.
LB2331.W523   1981   378'.125   81-2301
ISBN 0-470-27153-1   AACR2

Printed and bound in Great Britain by
Redwood Burn Limited
Trowbridge & Esher

CONTENTS

Was du ererbt von deinen Vätern hast,
Erwirb es wieder, um es zu besitzen.

(Goethe, 1832)

('What you have inherited from your fathers,
  acquire it again in order to possess it.')

For Margaret, who helped me take the wider view

NEW PATTERNS OF LEARNING

The Purpose of this Series

This series of books is intended to provide readable introductions to trends and areas of current thinking in education. Each book will be of interest to all educators, trainers and administrators responsible for the implementation of educational policies and programmes in higher, further and continuing education. The books are designed for easy access of information and contain bibliographies of key works to enable the reader to pursue selected areas in more depth should he or she so wish. This book is written by Dr John Wilson, Head of the Education Department at Moray House College of Education, Edinburgh. Dr Wilson's research in the area of student performance was published in *Degrees of Excellence* (1977) in association with Professor N.J. Entwistle. This book seeks to review the research evidence on student learning.

P.J. Hills
Leicester

ACKNOWLEDGEMENTS

I wish to express my thanks to the Principal and Governors of Moray House College of Education for granting me study leave in the summer term of session 1978-9 to enable me to prepare this book. It was thanks to Professor Karl Solstad that I was able to spend that time with my family in Tromso, Norway, and I am grateful to him and to the Norwegian University for making my stay there pleasant, stimulating and academically productive.

The social support and expressions of interest and encouragement one receives in writing a book are important, if seldom acknowledged, spurs to its completion, and I would like to extend a general thanks to all those who, at various times, and in a diverse range of settings, have enquired about its progress. I owe a particular debt to Dr Phil Hills for inviting me to take on this assignment and for showing forbearance at each passing deadline, to Noel Entwistle for many illuminating discussions on these issues of mutual interest, and to my colleague Chris Cumming who provided me with helpful, detailed comment on each chapter. Naturally, the end result is my own attempt to make meaning of a complex literature.

Librarians, secretaries and print department staff at Moray House College and elsewhere have assisted me in a great variety of ways. I am particularly grateful to two specialists in hieroglyphics, Mrs Elizabeth Innes and Mrs Lilian Lyall, who cracked my handwriting to type excellent first and final drafts.

I also wish to thank the following publishers and authors for granting permission to reproduce extracts from their publications: *Academic Press* and Alexander W. Astin; *Elsevier Scientific Publishing Company* and Noel Entwistle, Dai Hounsell and Maureen Hanley; Paul Ramsden and Gordon Pask; *Hodder and Stoughton Educational* and Noel Entwistle; *Holt, Rinehart and Winston* and William Perry; *University of Minnesota Press* and Douglas Heath; *University of Pittsburgh Press* and Roy Heath; *Scottish Academic Press* and J.B. Biggs; Ference Marton and R. Säljö; Gordon Pask, Leonard Svensson and Diana Laurillard, University of Surrey.

INTRODUCTION

In the past fifteen years, considerable attention has been paid by researchers to the topic of student learning. This work has an international flavour. In the United States, William Perry (1970) has put forward a stage theory of student intellectual and moral development; in Sweden, Ference Marton has examined students' approaches to the reading of complex prose; while, in England, Gordon Pask has reported a series of experiments on problem solving. Much of this and related work has become current in Britain through the influence of Noel Entwistle, who has edited (with D.J. Hounsell) a collection of readings on student learning and organised symposia on the subject.

This book is an attempt to bring together the various findings in one volume and, more importantly, to review their respective contributions to a theory of student learning. Such a theory could prove a useful guide to teachers, counsellors and others, including research workers, in planning the development of curricula and in undertaking focused research projects.

The book begins with an overview of general issues in the study of student learning (Chapter 1), and then explores the nature of meaningful learning in the arts and sciences (Chapter 2). Chapter 3 focuses on the context in which students learn and describes how students' perceptions of these contexts, and particularly assessment requirements, influence what and how they learn and the level of understanding they reach. Perry's work on students' intellectual and ethical development (Chapter 4) is next reviewed in the broader context of the 'impact' of college on students and alternative ways of conceiving of student growth. The role of the peer group in student learning is the specific topic dealt with in Chapter 5. Chapters 6 and 7 discuss the literature on how students tackle specific learning tasks; the former reviews the Gothenburg studies of Marton and his colleagues on 'depth' and 'surface' approaches to the learning task, while the latter describes Pask's work on the strategies which learners adopt to master complex subject matter. Chapter 8 deals with cognitive style, principally in terms of Witkin's dimensions of field dependence–field independence and Parlett's distinction between students who are 'syllabus bound' and those who are 'syllabus free'. Chapter 9 reports some of the current models of student learning and adds to these a model based on a developmental perspective, which represents the author's attempt at a synthesis of the literature. The final chapter sets out the implications for improving student learning in the context of teaching in higher education.

Every student is, of course, an individual undergoing a learning experience that is, for him, unique. Nevertheless, it is often possible to understand the individual better when he is portrayed against the background of general student development: if students and teachers know what kinds of intellectual qualities and attitudes they are trying to develop, they are likely to pursue these goals with greater determination.

The Main Questions Considered in the Book

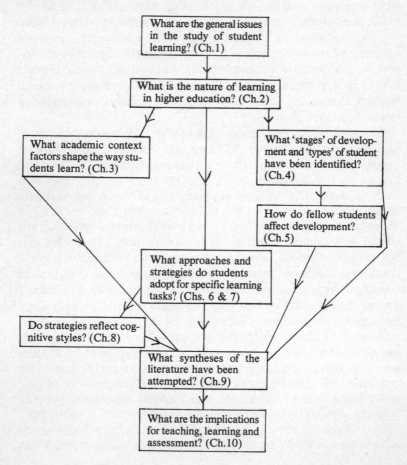

What are the general issues in the study of student learning? (Ch.1)

What is the nature of learning in higher education? (Ch.2)

What academic context factors shape the way students learn? (Ch.3)

What 'stages' of development and 'types' of student have been identified? (Ch.4)

How do fellow students affect development? (Ch.5)

What approaches and strategies do students adopt for specific learning tasks? (Chs. 6 & 7)

Do strategies reflect cognitive styles? (Ch.8)

What syntheses of the literature have been attempted? (Ch.9)

What are the implications for teaching, learning and assessment? (Ch.10)

1 APPROACHES TO THE STUDY OF STUDENT LEARNING

Students learn subjects and staff teach and assist them. We examine the efficiency of the arrangement by studying trends in degree examination performance. That may seem the obvious approach to the study of student learning, but it begs a number of important questions. One is the relationship between teaching and learning; another is how the characteristics of students and the nature of the subject affect what is learned. The study of examination performance, too, is fraught with problems: examination scripts may say as much about what students have *not* learned as what they have, and marks reflect the performance of the examiner as well as the candidate. Situations may have to be specially devised so that the process of learning can be studied. This chapter reviews the issues which will be discussed more fully in later chapters, and provides an overview of the literature on student learning.

The Relationship between Teaching and Learning

The purpose of teaching is to promote learning. The teacher's choice of teaching methods reflects assumptions about these purposes. Teaching in its broadest sense defines the framework within which learning occurs. Joyce and Weil (1972) have grouped the different patterns or models of teaching into four broad categories: (1) social interaction, (2) information processing, (3) personal development and (4) behaviour modification. The categories are overlapping, of course, and teachers may subscribe to different models according to their particular purposes. Some teachers may operate on a Skinnerian behavioural model, for example, stressing short-term and perhaps relatively transitory changes in knowledge, while others may pursue 'person' oriented objectives, such as Carl Rogers would advocate, involving deep seated changes in affect. A useful set of readings which illustrate some of the main differences between these approaches has been compiled by Entwistle and Hounsell (1975).

Many excellent reviews of teaching methods in higher education are available and a considerable amount of experimentation with new methods of personalised instruction systems has been reported (e.g. Beard *et al.*, 1978; Goldschmid, 1976; Gage, 1976; Hills, 1976; Wells, 1976). However there is little direct evidence on how and to what extent particular teaching methods promote student learning. Wells, for example, concluded a comparative review of the effectiveness of a variety of technologies and instructional methods with the observation that 'given favourable conditions pupils can learn from any instructional medium now available'. It is difficult to investigate learning from teaching because the criteria of 'effective' teaching are hard to define, and because teaching often involves a wide range of objectives not all of which can be assessed formally, or in the short term. Staff are often advised to base their teaching on a clearly defined instructional model (see, for example, Goldschmid, 1976; Gagné, 1976; Brown, 1978) but it is likely that relatively few staff are aware of this or plan their teaching accordingly. McLeish (1976) has the temerity to ask if there is any evidence that students do benefit from exposure to teaching, and facetiously suggests that one purpose of a lecture-based system of higher education (as in Britain) is to make students work independently to cover the ground missed by skipping the lectures! Researchers concerned with student lecture notes have been known to complain that such independent learning sabotages their attempts to forge the link between note taking and examination performance.

The crucial evaluation of teaching in higher education ought to be in terms of student learning. Instead most work has been reported on student preferences for different forms of staff-student contact, or their perceptions of the effectiveness of staff in their teaching roles. Studies by Beach (1960) and McLeish (1976) suggest that individual preference for particular teaching methods reflects personality factors. Pask's work demonstrates the importance of matching teaching style to the student's learning style: where students were mismatched very little learning occurred. The issues raised by matching are, however, complex.

The validity of student evaluations has been questioned by Thielens (1977). Whatever one's views on this issue the evidence is very strong (e.g. Percy and Salter, 1976) that students regard the teaching competence of staff as an important matter. There would appear to be a *prima facie* connection between 'good teaching', broadly defined, and the quality of students' work.

Students as Learners

Students are individuals with different needs and interests. Each has unique personal and social characteristics. They are also studying different subjects. The way each studies will reflect his perception of what he must do to meet the demands of the course: most students wish to graduate. Assessment, therefore, is of great importance. The student is also normally a member of a class. His perceptions may be influenced by hearing the opinions and advice of his fellow students. They may assist him in various ways, for example by defining the subject matter that is most important to learn, or by working with him in the laboratory or on a project. Students often teach each other (Goldschmid and Goldschmid, 1976).

The student may view learning in the short or the long term. 'Effective' short term learning may be signalled by the award of adequate grades. But what one comes to 'know' through a course is more than can be described quantitatively: candidates awarded the same class of degree may have acquired very different conceptions of their subject. Similarly, the significance of learning may not dawn until a course is completed, and even perhaps many years later. Courses have latent as well as intended effects. Vocationally oriented students may willingly conform to an unsatisfying academic regime, but they may buy their qualification dearly: a course which stunts the imagination and burns up its students' drive may lead to impoverished career fulfilment. Unimpressive finals performers often outshine their apparently better endowed contemporaries in careers after college. Relatively little research has been conducted on the long term effects of 'successful' adjustment to college, although several writers (e.g. D. Heath, 1978) argue that higher education must promote balanced development in the interests of 'maturity'.

Students are relatively homogeneous with regard to ability although there are considerable differences in intellectual power. Motivational and personality differences have, however, been reflected in level of achievement and approach to study. Students differ in the nature and degree of their interest in (a) study in general and (b) the particular task before them, and this may reflect their perceptions of the learning situation and the demands of the assessment. A sense of anxiety and feelings of self-worth may also affect how they tackle assignments and relate to staff. Entwistle and Wilson (1977) differentiated between students spurred on by 'hopes for success', and those who work neurotically, driven by 'fear of failure'. The latter were likely to be introverts, bound to the lecturer's definition of the syllabus, while the former were confident extraverts who carved out their own curriculum (in subjects where that choice was available), while studying strategically to cover the topics they deduced would be examined.

Interactions of personality and cognitive structures are often described as cognitive styles, such as 'field dependence' or 'field independence'. A large number of cognitive styles has been postulated (Messick, 1976) but empirical evidence for most is still lacking. Style is regarded as being relatively fixed, but it may be reflected in more flexible and specific strategies of thinking employed in problem solving. Information processing theory (Lindsay and Norman, 1972) suggests how students come to acquire specific subject matter, and postulates a 'dynamic' and 'integrative' role for memory, through which the mind creates new meaning. Bruner, too, stresses the active role of mind in transforming 'knowledge' into 'understanding'. He and Pask have highlighted the range of strategies which different students may call upon in solving conceptual problems.

Much interest centres on how students cope with the problem of mastering the massive body of knowledge they are set to learn. Some appear to have mainly a 'reproductive' or rote learning conception of study in which learning is equated with 'committing to memory'; others study with a view to extracting meaning from what they read, and relating general principles to their current stock of ideas and personal representations of reality. The distinction is often referred to as being between a 'quantitative' and 'qualitative' conception of learning.

Rote learning will be practised by all students at some times, and it may be a characteristic of study in fields such as modern languages or anatomy. Mnemonics and other aids to such learning (e.g. Morris, 1977) undoubtedly can prove useful. Studies by Marton and his colleagues have, however, suggested that many students adopt a reproductive or 'surface' approach to the study of reading materials even in situations where the task requires reading for meaning, or a 'depth' approach. They found, too, that surface processing was easier to induce.

Research on the characteristics of students as learners has led to the coining of many different terms. Parlett and his colleagues have contributed 'syllabus bound' and 'syllabus free' to the vocabulary, as well as the distinction between 'cue seekers' and the 'cue deaf'. McClelland's earlier work differentiated between students with a need for achievement (n ach) and those with a need for affiliation (n aff). Neurotic introverts approach study differently from neurotic extraverts. These poles or dimensions are undoubtedly useful in providing a way of conceptualising differences between students, but there are dangers in believing that they describe types of students rather than simply tendencies towards which students lean to a greater or lesser extent. Very little normative data exist to support the distinctions that have been advanced. Moreover, it is not clear how far the labels refer to separate or overlapping categories.

Underlying the use of such labels are wider questions about the predictability of the ways in which students go about learning. Do students approach different subjects and assignments in a recognisably similar way on each occasion, or do their perceptions of the task exert the predominant influence causing them to adopt situation specific strategies? The answer may depend on the evidence at which one looks. Certainly psychologists have studied individual differences in personality, motivation, cognitive style and strategies of learning in the hope that they would be able to identify factors which would be predictive of a consistent approach across different learning situations, and might provide the basis for general advice in counselling or study skills sessions. On the other hand, by focusing on the nature of each learning task one becomes aware that it presents a different problem for each learner. Its intrinsic interest, its importance for assessment, and its level of difficulty will be different for each student; successful coping will demand an individual response from each. Study skills advice, on this view, would only be useful in so far as it took account of the learner in relation to the task. In considering a model of student learning it is obviously important to establish which aspects of individual learning patterns are likely to remain stable, irrespective of the context, and which are likely to be responsive to the perceived demands of the task.

Another aspect of student learning is the scope of the effects of higher education on individual development. The aims of higher education include promoting changes in the values and attitudes of students. Before one can demonstrate the specific effects of higher education it would be helpful to have normative data on the effects of maturing on the population, but as Astin (1974) has pointed out, these do not exist. Two researchers who have contributed most to our thinking about qualitative changes produced by higher education are Roy Heath (1964) at Princeton and Perry (1970) at Harvard. Perry's scheme is Piagetian in that students are described as moving from a dualistic 'right-wrong' perspective on the world and learning, to a relativistic stance, and finally to a position of commitment to a consciously chosen style of life. Transition to each pattern involves trauma for the student and a re-shaping of his view of reality. Recently, however, such theory has been criticised for its self-fulfilling nature, and more specifically (e.g. Brown and Desforges, 1977) for the considerable evidence of *décalage* (limited generalisation of understanding to other tasks demanding a similar level of intellectual development). An alternative skills acquisition model of development has been advanced with its roots in information processing.

The Study of Student Learning

The psychometric tradition has exerted a powerful influence on the study of student learning. More recently the development within educational psychology and curriculum evaluation of alternative approaches to the study of the context of learning has been reflected in the definition of research issues. Elton and Laurillard (1979) have reviewed the weaknesses of traditional approaches and highlighted the strengths of the alternative and supplementary stances.

Many of the early British studies attempted to predict student performance by correlating ability and background characteristics and, in some cases, personality with the relatively 'weak' criterion of examination performance. Another interest was the comparison of the effectiveness of different teaching methods. Recent reviews of this literature are provided by Entwistle and Wilson (1977) and Beard *et al.* (1978). In the United States Cronbach (1967) emphasised the study of 'aptitude treatment interactions', i.e. the effect of variables such as a course of study on particular sub-groups sharing common characteristics. A considerable body of American research was concerned with the 'impact' of three or four years' exposure to higher education on the values and attitudes of the students, the criterion in most of the studies reviewed by Feldman and Newcomb (1969) being primarily changes in mean scores on attitude scales. Much of this research was undertaken with the aim of improving efficiency by reducing 'wastage' rates or increasing levels of performance, or justifying national investment in higher education in terms of benefits for society. These studies tended to assume that all students derived equal benefit from their stay on the campus, and that the relationship between entry characteristics and academic performance was direct and linear, often reflecting a cause-effect pattern.

An alternative to focusing on the 'impact' of college, or the 'products' or 'outputs' of higher education, is to view learning as a process whereby the student 'adapts' to the demands of the academic environment. 'Adaptation', indeed, implies a more passive role for the student than the results of process studies would justify, since studies such as Becker's (1968) and Miller and Parlett's (1974) indicate that many students actively pursue their own goals within the constraints imposed by their courses.

Several means of illuminating the learning process have been described. One is to explore how students conceive of their role, and how their conceptions are reflected in their approaches to study; another is to focus on specific learning situations, such as lectures and tutorials, and to observe how students behave with a view to explaining their actions; a third method is to observe how they tackle particular subject matter. Process studies focus on how individuals interpret the learning situation in which they are placed: they seek to describe situations from the standpoint of all the participants as a first step to explaining why some students cope effectively while others do not.

One can learn a lot by watching students study and asking them directly why they behave in the ways they do. But students are not always clear about their purposes, nor may they be able faithfully to describe how they thought through a particularly difficult learning problem. Another difficulty is whether it is legitimate to generalise from the student's description of how he tackles one or two assignments to a statement about his characteristic way of learning. Finally, there is the problem of the criterion of learning, which is often underplayed in process-oriented research: it is inappropriate to compare student learning directly when individuals may be describing their approach to different tasks on different courses.

An alternative methodology is to control the subject matter of learning and to study the variations in how students perceive it, relating perceptions to choice of strategy and testing 'understanding' formally in an examination. Pask has been the researcher most successful in externalising the different mental hypotheses learners have advanced to solve different conceptual problems, mainly in the sciences. But the question here is how far strategies employed in learning in ingenious, but often highly artificial, learning situations can be said to be typical of the way students would tackle the tasks they actually have to cope with in their courses.

Different approaches have their strengths and weaknesses: Elton and Laurillard (1979) make a relevant point when they note that results obtained in 'naturalistic' settings are qualitatively richer, but quantitatively less reliable, than those obtained under experimental conditions. Process studies provide data relevant to the interpretation of 'product' outcomes of higher education, while the 'audit' of academic performance is a public aspect of the process which neither staff nor students can ignore.

Conclusion

Research on student learning has moved from the search for general laws, such as Thorndike's Law of Effect and the Law of Exercise, to the study of how students vary in their approach to learning particular subject matter and problems. An identikit of student characteristics has been constructed from data collected by watching, talking to and studying students in natural and experimental settings. The purposes of higher education are so diverse that no single model can be expected to explain all learning. Problem solving, for example, may be defined in terms of the acquisition of skills on an information processing model, but it is doubtful whether 'self actualisation' could be explained on the same principle. Elton and Laurillard (1979) draw a parallel with the role of models in physics: mutually contradictory models may still, within their own terms, unify a range of concepts and evidence. Yet this does not preclude the search for common factors in how individuals learn.

This chapter has reviewed some of the issues and approaches to research on student learning. It may be helpful to summarise these, but it should be stressed that the different perspectives may require to be seen as complementary rather than as mutually exclusive.

Studies Which Emphasise ...

1. the impact of college on students *v.* the process of learning in college
   (e.g. entry/exit behaviour, 'pro-   (e.g. student adaptation to per-
   duct' or achievement data)   ceived demands of learning tasks,
                                      the nature of student-lecturer
                                      interaction)

2. consistency of student charac- *v.* variability of student behaviour
   teristics across diverse learning (e.g. learning strategies) within
   situations   situations

3. quantitative, reproductive con- *v.* qualitative concept of learning

cept of learning   as the search for personal meaning

4. learning in relation to the per- *v.* search for general laws of learn-
   ceived demands of the task   ing

5. student development conceived *v.* student development conceived
   as a progress through discrete   as skill acquisition generalised
   stages   across tasks

6. short- or long-term learning per- *v.* short- or long-term learning perceived from the student's point   ceived from the staff's point of
   of view   view

7. the intended effects of teaching *v.* the 'hidden effects' of teaching

2 THE NATURE AND PROCESS OF STUDENT LEARNING

'Facts are chiels that winna ding' is an old Scots way of saying that you cannot argue with facts. Every subject constitutes a body of knowledge, some parts of which the student has to master. On the other hand there is more to learning than merely acquiring factual knowledge. Whitehead (1962) summed this up in his celebrated remark that 'a merely well-informed man is the most useless bore on God's earth'. Learning involves understanding, and also caring (Peters, 1966). In this chapter I want to examine the distinction between what are often referred to as the quantitative and qualitative aspects of learning in terms of the processes by which students learn in the arts and the sciences.

Models of Learning

Holloway (1978) provides a useful framework for a discussion of the process of learning. He defines learning as the 'transformation of internal representations': learning may be said to have occurred if the mental processes by which one represents reality and internal understandings have been changed in enduring ways that are adaptive or advantageous to the individual, and not simply the results of maturation. Any learning situation involves an interaction of three factors: a task to be accomplished, a method of learning it, and a learner. Holloway suggests that the model of learning the teacher operates on will be reflected in the interaction of these three factors. One main distinction he makes is between an 'active' and a 'passive' model of learning. The passive model reflects behaviouristic assumptions about the process of learning, and is based on a static conception of knowledge as a copy of reality which has to be committed in its present form to the memory of the learner. On this view of knowledge the task of the learner is a straightforward one: he has to learn that an apple is an example of a fruit with certain defined properties, or that the organs of the body have conventionally assigned names. Such knowledge is objective, external and quantitative in the sense that the more you learn the better your chance of being regarded as a competent botanist or medical student. It can also be easily examined: the battle of Bannockburn was in 1314, and the Scots did beat the English. You either know this fact (if you are Scottish you do) or you do not. Such information can be learned passively, by rote learning, by stimulus-response techniques (as in the language laboratory), by association or by conditioning. In experimental learning situations where the task may be to memorise word lists or nonsense syllables the experimenter can manipulate the learner's interest by the provision of extrinsic rewards. Learning can be assessed, too, in terms of what the student has achieved, the time taken on the task, and the relative efficiency of different 'treatments': the criterion of learning is usually in terms of performance on an external test, often of the objective type.

In the active model of learning the structure of learning tasks is more complex and the main interest is in the process by which the learner reaches understanding of this structure. The laboratory studies of Bruner (1956) and Pask have explored how students come to master principles of classification with complex subject matter. The nature of the task requires the student to show 'understanding' based on his own exploration of the material. The learner, therefore, must be allowed to decide how he will learn. Onus is placed on the learner actively seeking out his own solution, and making his own integration of approaches. Assessment of performance will focus on the way the task has been tackled as much as on the learner's capacity to solve the problem.

Underlying the active model of learning is the view that learning, or coming to know, is an active process of mind on experience. This view has been expressed by philosophers and psychologists as diverse as Dewey (1917), Polanyi (1958), and Bruner (1960), but its two most influential exponents have been Piaget (1971) and Kelly (1955). Several useful introductions to their work are currently available (e.g. Donaldson, 1978; Fontana, 1977), but a brief account of the main aspects of their conceptions of learning may help to clarify further the distinction between quantitative and qualitative learning which has been the focus of much recent research on student learning.

Piaget (1971) sees intelligence as the way the mind organises reality: 'the essential functions of intelligence consist in understanding and in inventing, in other words in building structures by structuring reality'. 'Invention' therefore precedes 'understanding', and is 'the expression of a continual construction process building up structured wholes'. We 'know' an object when we act upon it (perceptually and mentally as well as physically) and transform it. 'To know is therefore to assimilate reality into structures of transformations, and these are the structures that intelligence constructs as a direct extension of our actions.' Piaget's functional view of the mind solves the problem of motivation: as an organ of the body, like the heart, the mind has its own instinctive functions to fulfil and derives satisfaction from the way it acts upon objects.

Piaget sees human learning as a process whereby the organism adapts to the environment by means of interaction:

> generally speaking, adaptation presupposes an interaction between subject and object, such that the first can incorporate the second into itself while also taking account of its particularities; and the more differentiated and the more complementary that assimilation and that accommodation are, the more thorough the adaptation. (Piaget, 1971)

Assimilation and accommodation are complementary and simultaneous; Elkind equates them with nature and nurture respectively, while

> reason — the process of intelligence — manifests an equilibrium between assimilative and accommodative activities and is thus relatively autonomous of both inner *and* outer forces. Reason guarantees that the mind and the environment will each retain their integrity in the course of their interaction. (Elkind, 1970)

One important question is the 'extent to which various mental processes are relatively autonomous from environmental and instinctual influence': in some situations, such as ritual or role playing, the accommodative process is dominant since the participant has to project himself into the situation of another, and speak and feel as he might; in others, such as symbolic play (writing poetry, perhaps), assimilation is dominant since it is inner needs which dominate, and external 'events' are arbitrarily used as props for the expression of mind and emotion. Equilibrium occurs only after a long period of restructuring in each stage of development. Development itself is a process whereby 'states of limited or partial equilibrium . . . are replaced by "better" states which are characterised by being able to handle a greater number of contingencies and by being more mobile, more permanent and more stable' (Donaldson, 1979).

Piaget sees two paths to mental growth. One is 'substitution', where less mature ideas are replaced by more mature ideas; the other is 'integration', where less mature ideas are synthesised to arrive at more complex and abstract conceptions. Mental growth through 'substitution' occurs most readily in spheres of moral judgement, consciousness, causality and religious identity. The young child may, for example, believe that everything that exists is conscious, that flowers are hurt when they are pulled, etc. As he grows older he differentiates between inanimate objects and conscious creatures, but an important point is that the less mature forms of thinking persist into adulthood. People may revert to them, as when they treat their car is if it were 'human', give it a name or kick it when it fails to start. Substitution of more sophisticated ideas for less sophisticated will only occur if the child is mentally ready for the new explanation.

'Integration' occurs in logico-mathematical development. It, too, depends upon readiness, but its key feature is that mature thought subsumes the less mature: the ideas of the prevous level become the building blocks for the next higher stage. A simple example is of the way the child learns to distinguish between 'left' and 'right'. He can do so in terms of his arms and legs before he can tell which side of the road a car is driving on: as he matures and interacts with the environment he acquires a more sophisticated concept which builds on and replaces his previous one. The change is qualitative in that the learner is developing a more sophisticated understanding of reality as he synthesises discrete factual information into more complete and meaningful interpretations.

Kelly's (1955) theory of personal constructs explains the way we come to know reality also in terms of our first-hand experience, which forms the 'assumptive realities' or implicit beliefs on which we base our actions. Fontana (1977) has defined a personal construct as a 'unit of meaning which contains all the perceptions, interpretations and evaluations which the individual attaches to a particular event, or place, or person, or set of persons'. We hold our constructs at different levels of awareness, depending on the extent to which we articulate them in everyday life, and often become conscious of them through perceiving disjunction between our implicit beliefs and those of the people we interact with. The most vivid illustration of this point is provided by Alfred Schutz (1971) who describes the experience of a 'stranger' visiting a foreign country and finding he cannot understand what the natives say. He is forced not only to study what they do, but also the implicit beliefs which underlie his own actions. Students entering higher education are like the stranger: they have deeply held constructs about what it means to learn, based on their school experience, and stereotypes of the 'student role' on the basis of which they act (e.g. Percy and Salter, 1976). But they quickly become aware of discontinuities between their reality and that of their teachers, and an important part of student learning is 'figuring out' the mental behaviours staff expect them to acquire and will reward.

Underlying the active and passive models of learning, then, are two very distinct ways of conceiving of reality. The passive model conceives of knowledge as factual, representational and quantitative. The active model also recognises the importance of facts, but it sees that the significance of facts is problematical: it is the meaning which we ascribe to facts which determines their importance. The battle of Bannockburn is a fact, although one can question such matters as the calendar by which its date is determined, but more significant is the ethnocentricism implicit in the way the fact is remembered and commemorated, and the wider political context then and now within which the event derives its meaning.

Moreover the way we represent our knowledge has important implications for how we come to understand reality. Bruner (1966) pointed out that the ability to conceptualise is crucial to learning: 'intellectual growth involves an increasing capacity to say to oneself and others, by means of words or symbols, what one has done, or what one will do'.

Language is the most important conceptual tool we possess. It both enables us to control and order thought, and to follow out systematically and logically a sequence of ideas. Pask views learning as a kind of mental 'conversation' in which one part of the mind advances hypotheses and proposals which are the subject of comment and modification by another part. But equally the language we have access to shapes our conception of the nature of the real world: Wilkinson (1971) pointed out that the Greek concept of 'atoms' shaped scientific thinking for 2,000 years until modern scientists broke away from the idea that they were solid and permanent 'objects' and regarded them as energy, as a process. Kuhn (1962) has drawn attention to the fact that we have no 'pure observation language': two persons with different conceptions of the solar system will, in all likelihood, see different events in perceiving the same sunrise: 'what you see depends upon what you look at, and also upon what your visual-conceptual experience has taught you to see'. It is important, therefore, to recognise that what we take for granted in our everyday experience is culturally determined, and that much of the factual 'knowledge' of subjects is simply convention, which can be justified because of its importance for communication.

The Assimilation of New Ideas

Students may acquire factual knowledge on a rote learning or 'passive' model, but if we follow the thinking of Piaget and Kelly they come to 'understand' primarily on the basis of their own reflecting experience, into which they seek to incorporate the new ideas they encounter in their courses. The difficulty they face is that they are set to study subjects which are essentially the personal constructs of social scientists, writers, philosophers, chemists and biologists who have formed these constructs on the basis of their attempts to understand and interpret reality. In every field of study the student is learning within what Kuhn (1962) refers to as the 'paradigm' of the subject: 'the entire constellation of beliefs, values, techniques, etc.' which constitute the disciplinary matrix within which a particular learned community operates. Intellectual leaders in a field of study serve their apprenticeship within such a field, of course, as the juvenilia of great writers testify. Piaget, for example, worked on conventional intelligence testing with Binet in Paris before branching off into his own productive avenue of research. Great scientists and writers perfect the tradition within which they operate, but the greatest revolutionise the conception of knowledge within their field, or speak in a strikingly original fashion to the conditions of their time.

Such innovations in thought are difficult, even for those who make them, to integrate into their total thought structure, and it takes many years for their ideas to become assimilated into the consciousness of the professional group within which they work. Perry (1970), for example, has observed that staff who wish to support students to 'a more sustained groping, exploration and synthesis' often are unable to sustain themselves in this new role as teachers; when the students make an 'error' then 'the older form of responsibilities imposes on the instructor the imperative of "correcting"'.

Similarly, at the level of the group, Kuhn (1962) suggests that a major scientific discovery is only properly assimilated when its implications for all the ways in which scientists think have been worked out, and this may take many years.

A discovery like that of oxygen or X-rays does not simply add one more item to the population of the scientist's world. Ultimately it has that effect, but not until the professional community has re-evaluated traditional experimental procedures, altered its conception of entities with which it has long been familiar, and in the process shifted the network of theory through which it deals with the world. Scientific fact and theory are not categorically separable, except perhaps within a single tradition of normal scientific practice. That is why the unexpected discovery is not simply factual in its impact, and why the scientist's world is qualitatively transformed as well as quantitatively enriched by fundamental novelties of either fact or theory.

These descriptions of the process of coming to terms with new ideas may parallel the student's encounter with the content and principles of his subject. Moreover, the deeper the student explores his subject the more he becomes aware of its uncertainties and the tentative nature of the hypotheses on which current 'knowledge' is based. The seeming solidarity of current definitions of the scope and content of the curriculum is largely illusory, as Bernstein (1971) has observed:

The ultimate mystery of the subject is not coherence, but incoherence, not order, but disorder, not the known, but the unknown; [but] only the few *experience* in their bones the notion that knowledge is permeable, that its orderings are provisional, that the dialectic of knowledge is closure and openness. For the many, socialisation into knowledge is socialisation into order, the existing order, into the experience that the world's educational knowledge is impermeable.

Learning in the Arts and Sciences

Learning in the sciences and technology is often seen to be more fact dominated than learning in the arts. It might be easy to assume that science students operate on a 'passive' model of learning and arts and social science students on an 'active' model. But such claims are oversimplifications. Witkin *et al.* (1977e), for example, have drawn attention to the 'broad gauge' nature of the humanities and social sciences compared to the pure and applied sciences: they include subject areas as diverse as philosophy, linguistics and mathematics.

Nevertheless, while there are differences in the nature of learning in these different fields, and the balance between 'active' and 'passive' models may not be the same, it is a serious misconception to identify the models with learning in a particular field of study.

Learning tasks in arts and social sciences characteristically involve elucidation of the framework of assumptions within which different writers operate: the student is asked to examine presuppositions, compare and contrast, analyse arguments and evaluate the adequacy of interpretations of behaviour or social trends. At Harvard, a typical student assignment runs:

> You have read the Bible and a book of Greek plays. Now write for us a 2,000-3,000 word essay comparing the concepts of wisdom and justice held by the authors of the Book of Ecclesiastes, the Book of Job and Prometheus Bound. (Perry, 1977)

In philosophy, as Tricker (1971) has pointed out, the student is presented with many different attempts to find a solution to a problem, none of which is entirely satisfactory: understanding the dimensions of the problem involves understanding the strengths and weaknesses of the most important of these. Textbooks review the contributions of different schools of thought and raise questions, not to promote consensus or agreement, but rather to stimulate thought. The nature of the exercise is well put in R.T. Hollingdale's (1968) introduction to his Penguin Classics edition of Nietzsche:

> To read Nietzsche, decisively to reject him, *and to know why* — that would be more to the point. More to the point still would be to see why he *could* be right, to see out of what mode of thinking such opinions as his can proceed, to see how many ways of thinking there are: in brief, to stop being parochial. Not knowing how to think true more than one sort of opinion is like never leaving the street one was born in.

Now getting 'on the inside', in R.S. Peters' term, of Nietzsche or any great philosopher or writer is no easy matter. In a sense one has to crack their code to get at their meaning. They imbue words with special significance. They seek to convey subtle nuances of inter-pretation. To communicate involves both the writer and his reader: the act of decoding the message and encoding it into one's own constructs. To understand demands the capacity to make a qualitative response to the total communication rather than simply a quantitative one in which facts and arguments are 'totted up' as if each was of equivalent weight. It involves transformation of one's thought structure to incorporate the new meaning.

While this type of qualitative response to personal interpretation of reality may readily be conceded as the nature of learning in the arts, it will perhaps be less easily recognised as appropriate for the sciences. Certainly many students conceive of the sciences as a field where there are 'right answers' and where learning is the equivalent of memorising. It is true that for much of the time the student is learning general laws and statements of initial conditions from which it is possible to derive conclusions. The subject matter is more factual and hierarchically structured than in the arts, and it is possible to map this out as Pask has done. Textbooks set out the current, conventional wisdom of the discipline: they describe the best theory and its applications, they do not set out to 'prove' the theory, or set forth alternative interpretations of the data, or discuss the kinds of problems current theory does not adequately deal with. Rather than, as at Harvard, two lecturers proving 'deadpan and without comment' two opposed theories of the age and origin of the earth, derived from identical data, in most courses the student is simply asked to learn the theory which the lecturer expounds. Kuhn (1962) describes the process of learning in science through working out textbook examples as follows:

> [Students of science] regularly report that they have read through a chapter of their text, understood it perfectly, but nevertheless had difficulty solving a number of the problems at the chapter's end. Ordinarily, also, these difficulties dissolve in the same way. The student discovers, with or without the assistance of his instructor, a way to see his problem as *like* a problem he has already encountered. Having seen the resemblance, grasped the analogy between two or more distinct problems, he can inter-relate symbols and attach them to values in the ways that have proved effective before. The law-sketch, say f=ma (Newton's Second Law of Motion) has functioned as a tool, informing the student what similarities to look for, signalling the gestalt in which the situation is to be seen. The resultant ability to see a variety of situations as like each other, as subject for f=ma or some other symbolic generalisation, is, I think, the main thing a student acquires by doing exemplary problems, whether with a pencil and paper, or in a

well designed laboratory. After he has completed a certain number . . . he views the situations that confront him as a scientist in the same gestalt as other members of his specialists' group.

Learning science, in this view, is learning within a defined framework: it is seeing the applications of formulae, and doing laboratory experiments, like Becker's (1961) Kansas medical students, which confirm well established results. In Kuhn's terms the student is learning the 'paradigms' at the base of current practice. But it is clear from the above that learning science is not simply 'pyramiding facts': it is about the acquisition of concepts such as 'distance', 'density', gravity', etc. To know the number of miles from Earth to Jupiter does not mean you have the concept of 'distance'. Hurd (1970) defines a concept as 'a synthesis or logical relationship given to relevant information by the student; it is a product of his own imagination, insight or reasoned judgement'. Moreover, concepts are more than merely collections or orderings of facts:

> a concept has a cognitive organisation transcending the meaning of its several components. For example, in the concept of density as a ratio of mass to volume, density emerges as a relationship formed by the learner. Essentially density represents a conceptual invention that goes beyond the observed data. When a concept such as density becomes a part of the common experience of people it acquires a name which makes it possible to share its class identity with others.

According to Hurd the two key factors in learning science are having sufficient background experience to see the relationship between what one is learning, and the reality to which it pertains, and skill in the processes of decoding and encoding which leads to concept formation. On the first point it is likely that many science students find great difficulty in making 'sense' of what they are studying: unlike the subject matter of the arts and social sciences, much scientific theory, especially as expressed mathematically, bears only a tenuous relationship to the physical reality. Kuhn (1962) tells us that it took almost a century to develop Atwood's machine which gave the first unequivocal demonstration of Newton's Second Law of Motion, and this and other examples testify to 'the immense effort and ingenuity that have been required to bring nature and theory into closer and closer agreement'. It is likely that many pupils emerge from school 'qualified' in science, but lacking understanding of the prerequisite facts and concepts underlying the definitions which trip easily from their tongues. Hurd's (1970) description of the process of concept acquisition emphasises the active role of the learner in decoding and encoding:

> forming a concept is a searching process, exploring an unordered collection of facts for similarities and differences, for organisational principles and for a meaningful integration. In the process of abstracting a common property from a body of information, the student looks for logical relationships, invents, constructs and tests them by noting which features characterise most of the data but do not represent other bits of information. The process is one of discriminating, categorising and evaluating in a cyclic manner, always striving to get a better coding or arrangement of the data.

Conceptualised knowledge 'provides hooks for grasping new knowledge' and results in economical learning.

Learning in the sciences, then, is no more than in the arts simply a matter of 'mugging up' facts, although this may be the characteristic pathology of the science student. Those who subscribe to the 'science is facts' view are guilty of the 'Man Friday' fallacy. They believe that learning science is like discovering one day what was not there before, as Robinson Crusoe found the footprints on the sand. But scientific discovery (and student learning is akin to discovery) involves learning to look at familiar phenomena in a different way: it is the re-interpretation of data with the use of new concepts which causes restructuring of meaning to occur, and this constitutes new ways of knowing, for the scientist and the science student alike.

Pathologies of Learning

So far I have presented an 'ideal' account of the nature and process of learning in the arts and sciences. But while the distinction between 'active' and 'passive' models of learning is useful for distinguishing between different research traditions in learning, it is important to remember that real life learning tasks are likely to involve both kinds of learning, either concurrently or at different stages in a course. Moreover the way the individual student actually sets about learning will reflect his personality, ability and other factors. These aspects, which affect his perceptions of the task in its academic context, will be discussed more fully in the next chapter, but at this point it will be useful, in the light of the earlier theoretical discussion, to describe some of the pathologies or abnormal patterns of learning students have been known to display.

Some students cannot learn readily because they cannot put their minds to their work: problems of personal identity, family, sexual relationships, etc. loom so large in their consciousness that they intervene between the individual and the learning task, so dominating his thinking that he may need to seek out assistance from counselling staff or the student health service. Other students *are* able to work, but some do so uncomprehendingly while others quickly acquire a general grasp of the 'arts' approach but fail to make the time to master the subject matter. The former may work very hard, but adopt a reproductive approach to study. They may learn many facts but fail to understand their significance: they may be unable to see the wood for the trees. They approach all learning on a 'passive' model, perhaps because of lack of ability, or because they hold a narrow conception of what learning in higher education involves. The second group — students who lack scholarship — may quickly learn the forms of academic discourse: they approach issues actively and critically and have well developed linguistic skills. But perhaps because of their personality and active social life, and their wide range of interests, they have neither the time nor even, in some cases, the inclination to undertake the passive learning which goes with mastery of the details of a subject.

It is possible to see these several pathologies as manifestations of the inability of these students to achieve the necessary Piagetian equilibrium between assimilative and accommodative forces.

It will be recalled from the earlier discussion that where assimilation dominates, the individual is driven by his inner needs; when accommodation dominates, the individual imitates but does not incorporate new ideas or facts adequately into his consciousness.

A large literature has developed on the subject of the personal problems of students (see, for example, part II of *Students in Need* (1978)). In addition to overt psychiatric illness, which affects about two to four per cent of the student population, there is, according to Lucas (1978)

a heterogeneous range of psychological and psychosomatic problems which fluctuate in duration and severity, and indeed in symptomatology, and affect a further ten to twenty per cent of the population. The first group, the overt illnesses, usually impair academic performances; the second group have a more complex relationship to academic work. Work-related symptoms, such as concentration difficulties, fears relating to work performance, and so forth, are often present, but actual attainment in examinations is not necessarily reduced, and may indeed be enhanced by certain types of neurotic drive.

In an interview study at Princeton, Roy Heath (1964) described students who resemble those in Lucas's second group as 'plungers'. Their mood at interview was unpredictable: sometimes they were sullen and depressed; at other times they bubbled over with ideas. Generally, however, they were preoccupied with personal problems and fantasies of disaster: for example, they always predicted that their marks would be lower than proved to be the case. The interviews had a cathartic effect because they provided them with an opportunity to talk about themselves, and so they tended to take the session over, jumping from topic to topic, apparently unable to control the flood of ideas that crowded into their consciousness. Heath sees a link between the plungers' personality and the way they think: they dissipate ideas with their disinclination to suspend action, and need to be helped to discipline their thinking.

Accounts of their work by counsellors (e.g. Wankowski, 1979) do suggest that many students can be helped to overcome transitory personal problems at relatively low cost. A considerable increase in counselling provision in Britain has been made in recent years. Wankowski (1979) has argued that special units should be set up attached to these services to help students to explore their learning problems and develop new approaches to study.

It is possible that a counselling approach might be equally successful with accommodative or imitative students who act on a passive model of learning. This kind of student will lack the capacity to re-interpret what he learns separately from the way he has learned it; he will certainly accumulate facts, definitions, formulae, etc. and perhaps commit these diligently to memory in a reproductive or rote learning fashion. But failure to assimilate will mean that these ideas sit uneasily on the surface of his mind instead of being embedded into his deeper structures of knowing: accordingly he cannot examine them from different perspectives or relate them to other viewpoints or criticise them. Such deficiencies will become clear in several situations: he will find difficulty in explaining what he has learned, except in a reproductive way, as he learned it; he will be unable to 'act on' the knowledge when he is asked to apply it in a new situation as in suggesting hypotheses for further investigation.

Perry (1977) describes a similar set of student behaviours, rather uncharitably, as 'cow'. He defines 'cow' as 'data, however relevant, without relevances', i.e. without awareness of the contexts, frameworks, etc. which determine the origin, nature and meaning of the data (or procedures). 'To write on the assumption that "a fact is a fact". To present evidence of hard work as a substitute for understanding, without any intent to deceive.' Perry is describing the characteristics of examination scripts, and every teacher will recognise the 'borderline' kind of performance to which he is referring. But although this is a universal phenomenon 'cow' is likely to be particularly prevalent in physical science where, as our earlier discussion indicated, students may find it especially difficult to derive the meaning underlying subject matter.

'Cow' implies 'bull' which British academics might describe as 'waffle'. Perry defined 'bull' as 'relevancies, however relevant, without data'. To bull is:

> to discourse upon the contexts, frames of reference and points of observation which would determine the origin, nature and meaning of data if one had any. To present evidence of an understanding of form in the hope that the reader may be deceived into supposing a familiarity with content. (Perry, 1977)

Perry tells an amusing story of how a mathematics student, 'the Abominable Mr Metzger '47' waffled for an hour in a test on 'Modern Perspectives on Man and Society' and was graded A– for an essay on Geoffrey Gorer's *The American People*, a book he had not even read. Moreover, the student had not enrolled in that course at all. The tutor did not spot the deception and commented: 'Excellent work. Could you have pinned these observations down a bit more closely? Compare. . .in. . .pp. . .' Playing the examination game, like conforming to the student image in dress and hair style, may be quickly learned: attacking the question to find inconsistency displays evidence of critical thinking which the examiner is known to be looking for, 'not forgetting to be balanced' in assessing claims and counterclaims, name dropping and inserting quotations whose relevance may be strained to fit the context — these and many more are part of the armoury of the accommodative student. 'Bull' is hard to detect:

although 'a certain creative judgment and a willingness to risk are required by any critical comparison of competing interpretations of data. . .the forms of independent thought are readily imitable by any bright student' (Perry, 1970). It is likely, though there is a dearth of evidence, that waffle is presented in pure science and mathematics just as it is in the humanities; certainly the nature of waffle in these fields is worthy of investigation.

Conclusion

This chapter began by distinguishing between 'active' and 'passive' models of learning. Both models are relevant for understanding how students tackle work in a course of study. The discussion of the process of learning in the arts and sciences has focused mainly on learning as an active process. It is assumed that the main learning task confronting the student in higher education is to make sense of complex subject matter. To learn is primarily to create personal meaning, whatever the field of study, by actively restructuring one's mental schemata to incorporate new data. Student intellectual growth may be depicted quantitatively in terms of courses passed and facts acquired, but qualitative changes in the conceptualising of reality are more significant. Parallels drawn with the ways in which teachers and scientists cope with new ideas in their disciplines illuminate the process whereby the mind grapples with the implications of its own discoveries. The concluding discussion of learning pathologies brings us back to the realities of learners and highlights the different ways they respond to the academic context. The 'plunger' is hardly able to face up to work; the conscientious but 'lost' student who 'cows' is unable to make sense of what he is learning and hopes that the examiner will look kindly on his display of factual 'knowledge' and thus compensate his lack of understanding; the student who 'bulls' is consciously trying to impress the examiner and to cover up his lack of scholarship. Learners perceive and respond differently to the learning context and the tasks it prescribes, and it is to a more detailed discussion of this aspect of learning that we turn in the next chapter.

3   THE CONTEXT OF TEACHING AND LEARNING

Students in higher education follow a diverse range of courses in faculties, schools or departments. Some 'learn at a distance' with the Open University, but the majority are in full or part time attendance on campus and may alternate study with work experience, placement or teaching practice. Whatever the setting they follow a programme which includes lectures, tutorials, practicals, assignments and examinations and enjoy only a rather limited freedom of choice as to what and how they will study. Most encounters with staff are in formal class settings, but more informal contacts may occur when a student seeks help with an assignment, or through clubs and societies, and such contacts are likely to increase as the student gets to know his tutors.

In thinking of the context of teaching and learning it is important to consider the nature of the individual's experience as a learner, and how that experience is interpreted. Malcolm Parlett has emphasised that:

> Teaching and learning involve far more than 'transmission and reception of knowledge' that can be elucidated by attending to 'inputs' and 'educational products' — students/pupils do not respond merely to presented content and to tasks assigned, but rather, they adapt to and work within a local teaching and learning milieu which embodies and transmits conventions, beliefs, and models of reality that are internalised, govern the total response to presented academic tasks, and influence profoundly the processes of socialisation and intellectual development. (Parlett, 1977)

Moreover, students are not simply acted upon; they make choices, take decisions and appraise each situation, seeking in the most economical ways to fulfil its demands.

The 'context of learning' comprises, then, the academic programme which the student is required to follow in different departments, with its expressed and implicit objectives, and the teaching, course organisation and assessment that are a means to its realisation. The context also includes the respective perceptions of staff and students of the programme and its purposes. From the student's point of view the most important fact about the learning context is likely to be that it provides the means through which he may gain an academic award. This he may value for itself (intrinsically) or for vocational or other extrinsic purposes. It is likely that students will invest much energy in defining what and how they have to learn and the kinds of behaviours staff will reward with high grades. But the approach adopted will reflect both personality and motivation and definition of the student role. Equally, student strategies will reflect to some degree the roles which staff sanction.

This chapter begins by describing some of the salient differences in programming in different faculties and departments, since students' conceptions of what it means to learn are likely to be shaped by the teaching environment and the staff-student interactions which follow from it. This leads on to a more general discussion of how staff and students perceive each other, and in particular what students think they learn from staff in formal teaching situations. Finally the literature on informal staff-student contacts is reviewed, in the context of a discussion of student learning strategies. Several major American studies (e.g. Becker *et al.*, 1961 and 1968; Gamson, 1966 and 1972; Snyder, 1971; Thielens, 1977) have contributed much to our knowledge about the role of the academic context in student learning. The most interesting British evidence has been provided by Miller and Parlett (1974) and recently Ramsden (1979). Most of the data to be reviewed have been collected by interview, questionnaire or participant observation techniques. They have identified different student perspectives on the academic and especially the departmental setting, and related such perspectives to behaviour and patterns of staff-student interaction. The data thus reflect naturalistic or real world academic environments, and give many insights into how students initially perceive these and seek to clarify and then to fulfil their demands. On the other hand few of the studies relate student perceptions of the learning context directly to the way students actually tackle specific assignments, or to the levels of academic performance they thereby reach.

The Academic Experience in Different Fields of Study

The objectives of higher education are likely to be reflected in the teaching and assessment context through which they are to be realised. In their major review of college 'impact' the Americans Feldman and Newcomb (1969) maintain that the primary goal of college is 'increasing each student's knowledge and intellectual abilities and dispositions', but colleges and individual departments are likely to see themselves as fulfilling functions which are as much vocational or social as intellectual. Institutions pride themselves on their distinctive traditions and ethos, as Watts (1972) has indicated in the context of a discussion of differentiation within British higher education. Eddy (1959) remarked, at the end of a survey of colleges in the United States, 'the atmosphere of a college is like mist: one can't put one's finger on it, but no one should be able to stay in it long without becoming thoroughly soaked'.

Science and technical departments are more likely to emphasise training goals, while arts and social science departments may stress moral goals. In colleges of education, as Shipman (1969) has shown, there may be conflict between the goals of 'academic' departments such as education and methods departments.

Students in different departments spend varying amounts of time in class, and the nature of these contacts reflects the particular field of study. Another important factor in the learning experience is the extent and manner in which departments programme students' private work. Wilson's (1978a) review of this literature showed that students in medicine and science spend around twenty hours per week in class, and this is about twice as long as students in humanities and the social sciences. The nature of this contact reflects the type of university, with Oxbridge students having more small group tutorials while students in Scotland are more exposed to lecturing. While some of the more marked differences between universities may have changed since the above data were collected for the Robbins and Hale Committees, the inter-faculty differences appear to be intrinsic to studying in particular courses, and there remains a world of experiential difference between reading 'Greats' at Oxford, and taking, let us say, Brewing at Heriot Watt.

Entwistle and Percy (1971) showed how the number and type of contact hours and the related assignments meant that students in arts and social science typically spent their time preparing for tutorials, writing essays or simply reading, while pure and applied scientists tackled set problems and wrote up practicals. Ramsden (1979) noted a marked difference in the 'need to read' between Lancaster students in an arts and applied science department: in the former only four per cent of the students agreed that class teaching provided 'nearly everything you need to know' for the course, compared with 61 per cent in the latter. Moreover he found that study strategies in science appeared to be more task-related than in arts: background knowledge was more important in the former and level of interest in the work set in the latter. There were interesting differences, too, in the amount of 'freedom to learn' preferred by students in different faculties. Students in arts and social sciences, where choice of subject matter might be expected to be wide, protested at the 'excessive formality of the assessment systems and the lack of flexibility in choosing assignments'. By contrast applied scientists, whose 'professional commitment and perceptions of clear assessment goals and standards' marked them out from other groups, wanted their tutors to put more pressure on them to help them get through the set work.

Mention of student perceptions of the learning environment brings to mind the large body of such research on the characteristics of institutions of higher education in the United States reviewed by Watts (1972) and Dressel (1976). Unfortunately, with their concentration on student perceptions of the total college environment, as opposed to the departmental, which is the context most students in Britain work within, these studies would appear to have little relevance here, and even in the United States opinion is divided as to whether they have helped our understanding of how students learn.

Gaff, Crombag and Chang (1976) at Leyden in Holland and Ramsden (1979) have, however, explored student perceptions of the different *departments* in which they study. Gaff reported that all students perceived their departments — chemistry, medicine, law and psychology — as highly impersonal, but there were still considerable differences in 'student-centredness', and this reflected the extent to which subject matter was 'person' or 'thing' oriented rather than departmental size or staff-student ratio. Students themselves, by nature of their choice of subject, were likely to find the degree of formality close to their expectations.

Ramsden (1979) identified the following eight dimensions of learning environments in his study of departments, including the School of Independent Studies, at the University of Lancaster.

Dimensions of Learning Environments

Relationships with students	Closeness of lecturer/student relationships; help and understanding shown to students
Commitment to teaching	Commitment of staff to improving teaching and to teaching students at a level appropriate to their current understanding

Workload	Pressure placed on students in terms of demands of the syllabus and assessment tasks
Formal teaching methods	Formality or informality of teaching and learning (e.g. lectures *v.* individual study)
Vocational relevance	Perceived relevance of courses to students' careers
Social climate	Frequency and quality of academic and social relationships between students
Clear goals and standards	Extent to which standards expected of students are clear and unambiguous
Freedom in learning	Amount of discretion possessed by students in choosing and organising academic work (Ramsden, 1979)

Students regarded the first two dimensions as of greatest importance for learning. They appreciated staff who developed effective rapport, showed enthusiasm, demonstrated the relevance of academic ideas to everyday life and, in short, motivated them; staff who went too fast, talked over their heads, or made a fool of them, were not only personally disliked, but were felt to destroy interest. Thielens (1977) suggests that students resent being made to feel dependent on staff. Relations between such perceptions and performance have still to be reported from Ramsden's study, but the Americans Centra and Roche (quoted in Solomon and Taubman, 1973) did find that students learn more than expected from their aptitude scores if instructors are accessible and interested in teaching and in students as people.

On the other of Ramsden's dimensions many departmental differences were apparent. Applied and natural science courses were, for example, perceived as having the clearest vocational relevance, offering least choice, and having staff who supervised students' work most closely.

The private workload adopted by students appears to reflect personal factors such as introversion, and institutional factors such as the imminence of examinations, faculty, year and type of course (honours or pass degree) and the demands of the subject and of the department. Thoday (1957) reported that Birmingham mechanical engineering students spent three-quarters of their private study periods doing course work, while electrical engineers in the same faculty spent just under half. The students' 'freedom to learn', therefore, may be circumscribed to varying degrees even within the same field of study, and this may affect student satisfaction and level of performance. Beard, Levy and Maddox (1962) showed how the academic programme in these two departments differed in such matters as the ratio of lectures to tutorials and laboratory work, and the time devoted to the main subject as compared with 'service' courses. These differences were reflected in level of achievement: success in electrical engineering was likely to go to the 'autonomously motivated learner', but, the authors commented, 'the more impersonal teaching methods, greater reliance on outside lecturers, and the small amount of work directly centred on the students' professional interests may, in fact, decrease the likelihood of autonomous work motivation'.

Wankowski (1973) contrasted the close, supportive relationships in sixth form with the impersonal, bureaucratic world of first year in higher education, and argued that heavy timetabling, highly theoretical courses, and teaching which fails to motivate students or communicate at their level of understanding may have important implications for commitment to study. This bureaucratic treatment may continue to be experienced in large second year classes, at least in Scottish universities, as Miller and Parlett (1974) demonstrated, but the nature of staff-student relationships changes as students specialise within a field of study.

Student Perceptions of Learning

The fact that students perceive the academic context in a particular way does not mean that it has the effects they necessarily claim. It is possible that students are not able to identify what they are learning from staff because they take too restricted a view of what it means to learn.

Several studies have suggested that both students and staff view each other in terms of oversimplified stereotypes. Becker (1968) at the University of Kansas and Entwistle and Percy (1974) report that staff see students as 'good' or 'bad', which often means 'motivated' or 'idle', much in the way school teachers do. Percy and Salter (1976) found that staff regarded higher education as providing students with the opportunity to acquire 'excellence'. By 'excellence' they meant the general ability to think critically and independently, and also the specialist competences of the subject. At the same time they acknowledged that few students would in fact achieve such excellence, and they doubted whether it could be taught. With regard to assessment, for example, staff award grades to reflect their judgement of a student's ability and the interest and effort he has put into doing the assignment. But their expectations are idealistic and unrealistic since they forget that for the majority of students social life, personal interest and vocational plans (which do not include a career in research or higher education) conflict with that simple dedication to academic study which staff imagine they have. Ideas of excellence and scholarship are not among the constructs through which the majority of students interpret and evaluate the process of higher education. At Aberdeen, Entwistle and Wilson (1977) reported that only ten per cent of the students identified with an 'academic' orientation to study, and the proportion of intrinsically motivated students is likely to be small on any particular task.

From the other side of the dais student criticisms of the quality of teaching in higher education are too well known to need detailing. Staff tend to underplay the importance of teaching, and it still has a low place in the academic reward structure in higher education. Percy and Salter (1976) suggest that staff see higher education as primarily a learning opportunity for the student, and do not regard their own fulfilment of the teaching role as being particularly significant. Students, however, see higher education as a teaching situation: their definition of excellence extends only to the quality of the teaching. The unforgivable sin is to bore the student. But what is interesting in this connection is Becker's (1968) observation that even good teaching is not commented on, or even noticed, by students. It appears that they become so absorbed with following a line of argument or exposition that its source becomes 'eclipsed'. A few 'outstanding' lecturers are widely acclaimed, but the 'average' performer is not seen to make much of a contribution to student learning and 'bad' lecturers are often simply dismissed as having no impact at all. A similar finding from study-skills courses was reported by Chibnall (1979) who drew attention to the way that students seemed unable to recognise what they learned from such courses, 'the experience simply becoming caught up with other academic experience and so not attributed to its source'.

An interesting study by Thielens (1977) explored the specific question of what students thought they really did learn from staff. He interviewed fifteen Columbia University freshmen at the beginning and end of first year, and asked them about learning both in formal lecture and tutorial situations and in more informal settings, such as when the student was discussing an assignment with his tutor. In almost 50 hours of transcripts 200 separate passages relating to instructors were identified, but in only one in nine of these did students refer to learning as something that was actually or might possibly be occurring, and in only one in eighteen was the lecturer clearly identified as the source of learning. It was clear, too, that in 33 instances specific facts, principles or attitudes were being assimilated by students, but only 8 of these were acknowledged by the students, while in 17 there were 'pointed signs that the students' conception of their interactions with teachers as well as their perceptual organisation of the episodes, had left out the learning which actually occurred'.

The students were full of enthusiasm for the knowledge and skills they were acquiring at the university, and acknowledged the contribution staff were making in a general way. Yet Thielens concluded that the students could not identify when they were learning because they equated learning with an end result, a product, and defined the most important role in learning as their own. Thus a student might remark that he had 'learned a lot' in a particular class, with the stress being placed on what had been achieved, not in the process of achieving it. Or again a student's remark, 'At first I didn't *get* the teacher's sarcastic *references* to conservatism' (Thielens' emphasis), implied that learning occurred because the student subsequently supplied his own framework of interpretation. The students' view of themselves as independent learners explained their preference for discussion classes as opposed to lectures, since these offered opportunity for student participation, but they did not view the tutor's role in handling the discussion as a significant factor in their learning. Similarly, with assignments, it was the tutor's role as grader that the students saw as salient, and not the decisive effects of his validation of their work.

When challenged students often admitted that they had learned a lot, even from 'bad' teachers. But they preferred to think of learning 'with' staff, rather than learning 'from' them. Instructors were at best facilitators (e.g. 'he gives you an idea' or 'he's helping me to write better'), but it was on their own role as learners undertaking specific assignments and examinations that students placed greatest emphasis.

It appears that students become more prepared to challenge the infallibility of staff, particularly with regard to assessment, as they proceed through a degree course. On the other hand staff make assessment more personalised as they get to know students better, and Miller and Parlett (1974) have shown how the student's track record can be an influential factor in the class of degree he is ultimately awarded.

The Hidden Curriculum

Whatever the student thinks about the effectiveness of his teachers he is likely to pay close attention to what they say as a guide to distinguishing between key and peripheral aspects of a course. Deciding what is important to learn in a course of study in higher education is often not so obvious as might be thought. The formal outline of the course in the university calendar or departmental handout may give little guidance as to the skills and knowledge the student is expected to acquire. Staff may stress different objectives and confuse the student, and the 'rewards' they actually give in terms of grades may be for qualities other than those they have formally stated. An apparently minor element in a course may prove to be a major obstacle to its completion because of a 'tough' marking policy by a particular member of staff.

Snyder (1971), a senior administrator at Massachusetts Institute of Technology, has suggested that the first year entrant is generally disorientated and needs to develop a 'cognitive map' of the campus. He may have to choose subjects and options within them without being clear about their implications. Moreover the content is likely to be extensive, and however hard he is prepared to work he will find that expectations of staff, as reflected in topic coverage, additional reading or follow up activities, are greater than his capacity to fulfil them. He will need to decide what is most important for him to study thoroughly and 'selectively neglect' the rest.

It may be thought that the obvious source of advice on this question should be the teaching staff, but it is not always possible to rely on what they say. In one study of students in medical school at the University of Kansas (Becker, 1961) staff advised first year students to follow a four-fold study programme consisting of reading the text books, attending lectures, laboratory work and reviewing their notes. The students were able and dedicated, working extremely long hours, but they still found the workload overwhelming. Selection of content on some principle had to be made, but students differed as to what it should be. One school of thought was that the really important material was what was stressed by staff in the teaching sessions, although the relevance of much of this material for being a doctor was often unclear. The other view was that perceived relevance to the future professional role should be the touchstone, irrespective of whether the material was stressed by the staff.

The students' dilemma was resolved at the first test six weeks into the course when the examined material was found to be that stressed by the lecturers. The reaction of the class was predictable: the majority of the students quickly redefined their learning task as being to identify what staff considered important and to confine their attention to learning that. Thus they learned to conform, although the apparent irrelevance of much of what staff stressed continued to annoy many of them. Subjects like biochemistry, for example, seemed to be too theoretical to be of much use to the prospective doctor, and laboratory experiments were often viewed as pointless. Becker gives examples of student delinquency where results in practicals were 'cooked' or 'answers' copied out directly from the textbook as students conserved time and energy for learning the really important materials.

Becker's (1961 and 1968) studies illustrate how students conform to 'make the grade'. On the American campus the approach to study of many students appears to be dictated by their perceptions of the quality of work they need to turn in to maintain their desired grade level. They practise 'situational adjustment', learning the requirements of social situations and what makes for success in them, so that they can turn themselves into the kind of persons the academic context demands. They seek the formal rewards of academic study but with a minimal investment of effort and interest.

The worrying aspect of student conformity in pursuit of grades is the model of learning to which students are required to conform. Snyder (1971) vividly portrays the effects of the pressures of study in his selective, competitive, elite institution. At entry students are idealistic and keen to learn, but their desire to study issues in depth is frustrated by the constant round of class work and preparation for regular fact-based tests and examinations which they must do well in to proceed to graduate school. The formal goals of MIT are to produce graduates who are critical and creative as well as knowledgeable, But the effect of the academic programme is to create a 'hidden curriculum' which dictates how students learn,

> wastes human potential, blunts and distorts natural curiosities, de-emphasises creativity, individualism and responsibility, to make the individual more malleable. . .The student becomes a seller of desired goods, the professor is the consumer, with rewards paid in the relevant currency of grades.

The 'hidden curriculum', in short, is the kind of routine, fact-dominated learning the student really has to engage in to get the good grades necessary for success on the course; paradoxically students are highly likely to fail if they actually adopt the thoughtful, critical stance staff say they are trying to promote. Not surprisingly, therefore, many students withdraw emotionally from the course; others drop out either because of pressure of work, or because they find the course so boring and unsatisfying that they cannot endure it.

Informal Student Learning

The evidence reviewed in the preceding section suggests that students learn to distinguish between the formal and actual goals of a course, and to conform to its academic demands. One of the most powerful factors which motivates students to seek out staff is the need to clarify the basis of assessment.

In higher education each department has autonomy as to the particular pattern of assessment it adopts, within certain broad faculty policies. The requirements of each course have, therefore, to be separately identified by each student. Since students follow different courses and combinations of subjects and have different strengths and weaknesses in particular subject areas, as well as different levels of interest, the assessment requirements are unique for each. Of course, students will share perceptions and jointly discuss how to tackle particular assignments, or speculate as to the kind of questions they will be set in examinations. In some situations, too, students can learn from the experience of previous year groups, but there may be little communication between students, and the circumstances of teaching and assessment are likely to change over time. The student, therefore, has to identify as clearly as possible both what he has to learn and what are the mental qualities he is expected to display, if he is to tackle the assignments successfully. Such apparently minor factors as who sets the questions, or marks them, become important concerns in student thinking, and many students devote a great deal of energy identifying this kind of incidental information which may have major importance for the way they go about performing the tasks they are set.

Students in fact appear to display different degrees of 'strategic' behaviour in finding out about the assessment practices in particular departments. Nearly all can be expected to look over past examination papers, for instance, but beyond that there may be wide individual

variations which may reflect role conceptions and personality differences. At one extreme are students who are apparently 'cue deaf'
(Miller and Parlett, 1974). These students define their task as simply
to learn the syllabus; they are poor question spotters and do not
perceive hints dropped from staff which other students may seize on to
guide their revision. Moreover they appear to take the view that
question setting and marking are undertaken by some invisible college
of academics: they do not entertain seriously the possiblity that the
impressions staff form of them as individuals may influence the way
they mark their work. At the other extreme are students who seek
short cuts to academic success by a variety of means which border on,
and in some cases exceed, what is legitimate. Becker (1968) describes
how some construct and work to a 'system' or hypothetical model of
how they will be examined. Others 'apple polish' or 'brown nose' by
chatting up staff and raising questions about the course, trying to
impress staff with their interest and width of background reading. At
the same time they exploit these informal contacts to probe the
qualities the lecturer is likely to reward. Miller and Parlett (1974)
identified similar 'cue seeking' behaviour among final year physics
students at Edinburgh University. These students were distinguished
from others who were simply 'cue conscious' by their active, questing
behaviour. They were keen to be known as alert and enthusiastic
students, and would take the lead in class discussions and buttonhole
staff after lectures or over coffee, discussing the issue of the moment,
but taking the opportunity, when the conversation moved on, to raise
questions about the subject matter, the topics most likely to feature in
the examinations, the expectations and idiosyncrasies of markers,
and the name, interests, publications and preferences of the external
examiner. Cue seekers acted on this information by concentrating
their revision very largely on the topics they had identified as virtually
certain to come up. They even practised writing out the kind of
answers they would give, taking care 'to be balanced' if that was the
slant the marker was likely to be looking for. They saw examinations
as a kind of 'game': the important thing was to acquire the correct
techniques. Cue conscious students, on the other hand, while alive to
the fact that staff dropped hints, took a more cautious approach to
revision, selecting a wider range of topics which they studied in less
detail, and trusting for success both to hard work and luck on the day.

There is, of course, always an element of risk in self promotion.
Cue seekers may be regarded as egregious by some staff, and in some
departments the policy may be that 'lips are sealed' with regard to

information about examinations. Miller and Parlett in fact found considerable individual differences between staff on the matter of hinting, while Ramsden (1979) reported one technology department where staff were sworn to secrecy, although the students still claimed to be able to distinguish between the answers they thought were 'right' and those that staff might expect them to give.

Certainly the cue seekers' strategies appeared, on the whole, to pay off. Three of the five students in this category in Miller's study were awarded firsts, compared with only one of eleven cue conscious and one of fourteen cue deaf students.

Students, then, may seek to manipulate informal contacts with staff in order to maximise their chances of academic success, but the nature and extent of such contacts may reflect such factors as staff role conceptions and the stage of the course students have reached. It is possible, too, that the pattern of interactions can have implications for the curriculum and academic standards.

Shipman (1969) provided some evidence in a study of staff-student relations at Worcester College of Education. Worcester was established at the end of World War II. It was a small, close-knit college with a high intake of ex-service personnel who were very keen to teach, but relatively uninterested in the academic and professional elements in their training course. The staff found that the close personal relationships they had established made it hard for them to be severe with them, and so they defined the academic standards at a level the students were capable of reaching. Teaching competence, too, was defined in terms of 'personality' rather than formal academic achievement.

A study by Gamson (1966 and 1972) provides interesting sidelights on departmental differences in the closeness of staff-student relationships and their implications for the curriculum and academic performance. Gamson interviewed 33 staff and some senior students who had taken natural and social science courses at Hawthorn, a small residential liberal arts college, four years after it had opened. The staff in the two departments were conscious that they had different expectations of and relationships with the students. One remarked that the departments were 'as different as night and day...we frustrate each other and confuse the students'.

The natural scientists adopted what Gamson (following Etzioni, 1961) terms a *utilitarian* orientation to students: they taught courses which were formal, highly structured and impersonal, maintained social distance, and emphasised cognitive achievements and high standards of performance. They attached little importance to promoting the students' identification with college. The social scientists, on the other hand, displayed a *normative* orientation: their courses included many options which permitted small group or individual tuition, and they encouraged students to interact with staff as equals.

Personal contact was sought after mainly by members of the student 'leading crowd', but a substantial minority did not wish to participate. Within the staff, too, different sub-groups emerged sharing to a greater or lesser extent the dominant ideology: several social scientists saw their role, for example, as one of radicalising the students. But it was not long before staff in both departments found it difficult to accept the implications of their own teaching. The criteria for grading were a headache for the social scientists as was what to do about delinquent students who cut classes or overran deadlines for the submission of work. They were outraged when students challenged the legitimacy of the curriculum they had devised for them. Their emphasis on personal contact and critical attitudes, in short, undermined their authority by creating role conflict within the staff, and inevitably they were forced to move towards a more utilitarian orientation, a process speeded up by the departure of many of the radicals.

The corollary of the natural scientists' emphasis on high grades was high failure rates. The students consequently exerted pressure on staff to modify the curriculum and set standards the students were capable of reaching. The staff compromised, not by offering more personal support on a normative model to help students reach the initial target, but by lightening the curriculum and lowering the standard.

It is possible that different patterns of interaction may reflect the orientations of staff and students. Typologies of staff and students have been suggested by Clark and Trow (1966). The staff typology relates identification with college (local or cosmopolitan) to commitment to teaching or research and describes staff as either (1) local teachers, (2) scholar-researchers, (3) demonstrators or (4) consultants. The student typology (see Chapter 5) identifies four sub-groups of student — (1) academic, (2) vocational, (3) collegiate and (4) nonconformist. Interaction patterns for these different 'types' would be likely to vary: 'local teachers', for example, would probably be most accessible to students, while 'consultants' would rarely be visible on the campus. The proportion of staff falling into each of these categories is likely to depend on the institution. Vocational students are likely to be particularly anxious to define the assessment requirements of the department, while academic students might seek to interact with scholar-researchers.

Conclusion

This chapter has reviewed evidence on how the departmental context affects student learning. It has shown how the academic programme shapes the student's experience of learning and can affect his academic performance. Students certainly report that they are better motivated to learn if staff appear to be interested in them as individuals, and if the teaching is stimulating and provides support as well as variety and challenge. Even at MIT, as Parlett and King (1971) demonstrated, changed teaching methods led students to report 'better' learning.

Students have to define what and how to learn. In most courses there is likely to be some gap between the formal and actual goals of teaching. Students will conform to fulfil the demands of the assessment. They may study strategically in the light of evidence they have gleaned from informal contacts with staff and from being alive to the hints staff drop. Students who strive to impress staff, and who seek out information about assessment, do appear to do best. Feldman and Newcomb (1969) also reported that the ablest students had most frequent interactions with staff. There is some evidence that cue seekers benefit from making themselves known to staff, but they appear to be impressive students in their capacity for hard work and commitment to study. Hounsell and Ramsden (1977) also remarked on how their strategic students

> had the ability to see the assessment tasks in the wider context. . . they tended to be the students who approached their work in a very positive way, trying to see connections between previously studied and currently studied materials, relating specific tasks to their general understanding of the subject area, and relating their reading or problem solving to their own extra-curricular experiences. Most lecturers would regard these approaches to academic work as characteristic of the better student.

It may be, then, that cue seeking is an expression both of intrinsic motivation and commitment to study, as well as of greater self confidence as an independent learner. Miller and Parlett, in fact, compare these students directly to Perry's (1970) committed students, and there are parallels with Entwistle's confident extraverts.

A lot of the evidence reviewed in this chapter suggests that students invest much time and energy learning how to be conformists. Yet if Becker and Snyder are to be believed they are trained to play the system, or to 'accommodate', and to produce work which has the appearance of scholarly performance without the substance. Unfortunately the British evidence is none too hopeful either. Entwistle and Percy (1974) suggested that staff reward conformity rather than creativity: 'lecturers who talked of their aim to stimulate students to think critically in practice constructed courses, and taught, in terms of bodies of knowledge that a student should acquire to deserve his degree'.

Both Becker and Snyder argue for abolishing grades, or shifting to a simple pass/fail system, but such solutions are unlikely to draw a positive response from the academic community, and it has been suggested (e.g. Sarafino and Dimattia, 1978) that undergraduate achievement is lower under pass/fail. But if grades cannot be abolished it should at least be ensured that they are earned in a genuinely educational manner, and this implies better teaching and assessing and imaginative curriculum development. Snyder warns of the 'ecological trap' in higher education: short term 'adaptation' to the demands of the pressurised work load of an institution like MIT may blunt the qualities of curiosity and creativeness which are necessary for subsequent fulfilment.

Students in higher education are on the threshold of independence. They appear to think of themselves as independent learners, but to undervalue the contribution their teachers make to their development. To some extent, of course, staff connive at this student image by stressing that higher education is something the student has opted for. The nature of interaction with staff depends on the academic programme and also on how staff and students define their role. But the quality of staff-student relationships can have implications both for student support and survival and for the curriculum and academic standards.

Gamson suggests what is perhaps the ideal compromise: 'not so harsh a concern with academic standards as to smother a close connection between student and faculty, and not so intimate a connection between student and faculty as to undermine academic expectations and demands'.

4 THE MORAL AND INTELLECTUAL DEVELOPMENT OF THE STUDENT

If a student were asked to describe how he was 'getting on' with his studies he would probably reply in terms of the year he was in, the number of degree examinations or subjects he had passed, or the part of the subject he was currently specialising in. Such an answer, focusing on the external or quantitative aspects of his progress, would provide little qualitative information about developments in his epistemology or in his perception of his role as learner. It would tell us little about the changes that had occurred in his personal values and ideals, in his conception of the purpose of study, or in the ways in which he had developed new and more effective techniques for reading textbooks, writing essays or thinking about the subject matter. In many respects, however, these are likely to be the most significant and enduring products of his years of study, although even he may not be fully aware of them at the time. For all the importance attached to examination performance in higher education, it is curious that no follow-up study appears to have been attempted ten, twenty or thirty years after graduation to see how much of the substantial body of factual knowledge acquired over a course actually is retained. Perhaps this coyness of researchers reflects fear of non-co-operation, or perhaps the results would be too embarrassing to report!

The evidence reviewed in Chapter 2 suggested that the study of a subject involves the creation of personal meaning, and exploration of underlying moral issues. Many staff may regard the account presented in the last chapter as a caricature of the realities of staff-student contact: they may believe that through their teaching they have a profound effect on the way students come to think about their subjects and, more widely, about themselves in relation to the society in which they live. Education at any stage has important moral purposes and both the curriculum and administrative arrangements, such as residence, in higher education are often planned with the deliberate aim of promoting moral development in students (Plumb, 1964; Collier *et al.*, 1974).

But what kinds of changes actually are brought about by study in higher education? How far do students grasp the fundamental principles of their subjects? What point of contact do they see between 'academic' issues and wider political and social problems in contemporary society? What are the moral effects of studying particular subjects? Does the study of literature make students more 'sensitive', and is this shown in their interpersonal behaviour? Does the study of science lead to a respect for truth and evidence, and does this shape their general attitude of mind?

These and similar questions are extremely difficult to investigate in the short or long term. Yet an evaluation of the effects of higher education on students cannot ignore them. It is to American research that we must look for such evidence as is currently available.

Methodological Issues

The standard way to measure student learning in most institutions is by means of formal assessments in traditional degree examinations or open-ended assignments such as dissertations. Such techniques may or may not be effective means of measuring cognitive development, but they are very indirect and probably inadequate for measuring the development of attitudes, character and values. In some studies instruments such as the Study of Values or the Omnibus Personality Scale (OPS) have been used to try to measure these aspects of student growth; others have relied on interviews, participant observation and case studies.

The use of different techniques reflects different ways of conceptualising the problem of measuring 'effects'. One approach, emphasising a traditional psychometric methodology, has sought to measure the 'impact' of college on students by means of 'before' and 'after' studies, building in controls from comparable groups of non-college attenders where possible. Observed changes are usually reported in terms of mean scores and standard deviations which are explained as the 'effects' of college attendance or of particular programmes. An alternative approach has focused on the process of interaction of the student and the college experience, both describing and interpreting student perceptions. The most influential work so far reported from this standpoint is by Perry (1970) who takes a developmental perspective on intellectual and ethical development. His views have been criticised, however, by those who see development in terms of fulfilment of the individual's intellectual, social and emotional selves.

Before proceeding to review these studies let us consider Astin's (1974) discussion of the methodological problems of research on college impact, in which he sees three conceptually distinct components as relevant (see Figure 4.1).

Figure 4.1: Model of Factors in College Impact

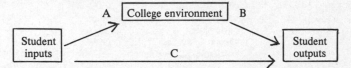

Student *inputs* comprise those talents, skills and potentials for growth and learning that the new student brings with him to college. Some student inputs are ascribed characteristics, such as sex and race; others reflect the student's present level of intellectual development and personal values. Students are likely to differ in maturity, level of moral awareness and commitment at entry to a course.

The college *environment* refers to those aspects of the institution that affect the student, for example, its administrative policies, its physical plant and facilities, its curriculum, including methods of teaching, and the individual's peer group. Departments and individual staff are likely to have different conceptions of their role with regard to moral development.

Student *outputs* consist of those aspects of the student's development influenced by the institution and will include the academic achievement, knowledge, values, attitudes and interests, which universities and colleges more or less consciously are seeking to develop. The very range of such impacts suggests the wide scope of any study seeking to give a comprehensive picture of institutional effects.

Astin (1973) suggests that two types of data may be collected for measuring output in the cognitive and affective areas — psychological (test results and attitude scores) and behavioural (actual choices made or decisions taken) (see Figure 4.2). Such data may be collected both in the short term (end of course) and long term (mid-career).

But it is perhaps rather naive to conclude that institutional effects will be either positive or simply not present: it is possible that negative effects may also occur. Ellison and Simon (1973) suggest that impact studies should consider the role of college in developing such qualities as courage, the capacity for effective leadership and followership, Machiavellian skills, competitive skills, cut-throat types of behaviour, the capacity to exploit intellectual style and jargon, to rationalise, deceive and be deceived and to relate to people of very different

Figure 4.2: Measuring Outputs in Higher Education (Astin, 1973)

Type of data	Cognitive	Affective
psychological	knowledge	self concept
	general intelligence	interests
	critical thinking ability	values
	basic skills	attitudes
	special aptitudes	beliefs
	academic achievement	drive for achievement; satisfaction with college
behavioural	level of educational achievement	choice of major
	voc. achievements; level of responsibility, income, special recognition	avocations (e.g. time spent on recreation)
		mental health
		citizenship (e.g. community participation)
		interpersonal relations

backgrounds. Effects, too, may be indirect, and interactive, as well as direct: the relationship between 'being failed' and mental illness, for example, may raise complex questions of causality.

Astin's model in Figure 4.1 highlights some of the factors impact studies need to consider. The main aim is obviously to assess 'B', but 'C' reflects the fact that we must take account of changes that are happening to young people between the ages of 18 and 22 anyway, viz. that they are growing up and maturing. Unfortunately there is little normative data on late adolescent development to enable us to make direct comparisons. 'A' draws attention to ways in which the student body is unique to each institution. Simple conclusions may not be warranted: thus the lowering of religious affiliation amongst college students may be typical of the country as a whole and not a particular feature of the experience of college. Reporting of group mean scores and standard deviations may mask significant individual changes both towards and away from the desired growth.

Studies of College Impact

The major review of impact studies in the United States is by Feldman and Newcomb (1969). Although changes are identified, most of the studies exhibit the weaknesses in design that Astin (1973) has alluded to. Results on the Study of Values Inventory or the OPS suggest that students attach increased importance to aesthetic values, and decreased importance to religious values, between first year and fourth year. Students increase in open mindedness, decrease in conservatism (on public issues), increase in intellectual interests and capacities, show increased independence, dominance and confidence and a readiness to express impulses. Several of the studies take no account of the attenuation of samples through dropouts, fails and transfers. On the former point Huntley (1972) has shown how controlling for major subject of study can highlight value changes. Another finding is that students in different fields have been shown to differ in value orientations, with science students high on theoretical, medium on economic and low on aesthetic values, while arts students are medium/low, low and high respectively, but it is possible that these differences were present on entry.

The one study to highlight permanent institutional effects on values was Newcomb's (1943) investigation at Benington. Benington in the 1930s was a small, residential, private, female liberal arts college with a staff espousing rather radical values. The students came from traditional middle-class WASP (White, Anglo-Saxon, Protestant) backgrounds. Four factors seem to have been influential in promoting value change among the students at Benington: (1) the goals of the institution were clearly and explicitly stated; (2) there was consensus amongst the staff as to the goals to be pursued; (3) the institution was autonomous and detached from the pressures of its neighbouring environment; and (4) it was small enough for staff and students to interact continuously. On a follow-up of Benington graduates in the 1970s Newcomb found that most had remained true to the liberal ideas they had learned in college. Many of the students had kept in touch (some, indeed, had married the brothers of their contemporaries). But Benington had changed in the 1960s: its high reputation for liberalism, enhanced by the publicity given by the Newcomb study, had resulted in it attracting students from liberal backgrounds who were already in tune with the values of the college: in this way it can be seen that the impact of colleges may be reduced as the nature of that impact becomes known.

Two longitudinal studies of college impact in the United States have been reported recently. The Cooperative Institutional Research Program is an ongoing survey (Astin *et al.*, 1979) of entrants to higher education. Since 1966 one in six of all college freshmen has supplied 150 items of information on social class, high school achievement, attitudes and aspirations. Data for more than two million students in more than 500 institutions have been collected. Trent and Medsker (1968) followed up 10,000 high school seniors from 1959, testing with the OPS. They found that the attitudes of students from 'emotionally rich' family backgrounds (i.e. backgrounds characterised by autonomy, liberality and flexibility of thinking) changed more often and to a greater degree than those from impoverished family backgrounds. Another interesting finding was that the general level of dissatisfaction with life (and especially career) was very much higher for those who had not attended college, yet these individuals refused to acknowledge that they needed additional education if they were to achieve their career goals. Significant, but small, changes in cognitive level and personality were reported in the following areas: increased aestheticism, greater complexity of thinking, higher religious tolerance, decreased political naïveté, increased impulse expression, decreased stereotyping of sex-typed interests, and more realistic setting of goals and aspirations. The magnitude of the changes was found to reflect exposure to college, being greater in college persisters and smaller in withdrawals and non-college attenders. Least changes were found amongst non-college women who had borne children. Students also reported an increase in such activities as browsing in book stores, concert attendance and reading.

What does seem to emerge from the literature is the accentuation of differences between students in different fields, but it is not clear why such accentuation occurs. One theory is that it is a sign of 'progressive conformity' where students tend to change in the direction of their fellow students' dominant characteristics. It is possible, however, that the changes may merely reflect the increasing sophistication of students who recognise the 'socially desirable' responses. Several interpretations are possible. Indeed the weakness of impact studies is that they do not help to explain how growth occurs: the student is conceived of as a passive recipient of the learning mediated by his teachers who themselves are assumed to pursue consistent objectives and goals which they seek to realise in every student equally.

Institutions certainly have effects on their students, inducing changes that would not otherwise occur (e.g. gain in subject knowledge) or exaggerating or accelerating changes already occurring. Equally they may impede or counteract changes resulting from other sources, such as when effective teaching convinces a student that he can master statistics when his impulse is to drop it. But it is difficult to demonstrate what Watts (1972) has termed the *intrinsic* effects of an institution, i.e. the change it actually brings about. It is important to remember Thomas's (1932) dictum in this connection — 'if men define situations as real, they are real in their consequences'. If an institution, such as Oxford, is believed to have an impact on its students' thinking and outlook, employers will be well disposed towards that institution's graduates and give them preference over other graduates. Thus it is the image of the institution, the beliefs about its ethos and how it shapes learning and character, that will be influential. It is easier to make claims about institutional ethos than to substantiate them.

Paths of Student Development

An alternative to studying the 'effects' college courses have on students is to consider how students react or adapt to college experience in the light of their own path of development. One view is that student growth occurs through an invariant sequence of stages or levels in which progress from stage to stage implies a restructuring and reorganisation of what went before. 'Higher' stages are qualitatively different from 'lower' stages in terms of the way the individual thinks, feels or acts. Another influential view is that student development is to be seen in terms of mastery of a series of developmental 'tasks' which involve the individual's maturation in the different aspects of intellect, emotions and social relationships. On this view the effects of college may be studied in relation to the way that each aspect of personal growth is promoted or retarded.

(a) Stage Theories of Student Growth

Many psychologists have advanced stage theories of development in childhood and adolescence. Parker (1978) defines a stage as 'a pattern of behaviours that is distinctly different from the patterns of other stages: the individual so orients towards life that his or her responses have a particular recognisable consistency'. Since development is in fact continuous, stage theory simply catches a snapshot of the individual at a particular point of time. The concept of stages is useful for describing different aspects of the individual's personal characteristics and to differentiate between age levels. But Muuss (1968) has pointed out that 'no exact agreement exists among the various stage theories as to the number, characteristics and psychological meaning of each of the stages'. Stages are not clearly differentiated, may occur at different ages in different cultures, and progress from stage to stage is not uniform in all aspects of the individual's thinking or behaviour. Nevertheless there does appear to be consensus that development follows an orderly progression, that the stages are qualitatively distinguishable and, notwithstanding the descriptive accounts provided, that movement from lower to higher stages is the preferred path of development. Stage theory, therefore, implies a 'deficit' model of development, in that the individual moves from less to more complex interpretations of the world through the stages.

Tomlinson (1974) provides a useful review of psychological theories of moral and intellectual development over the college years, summarising the work of Kohlberg (1969), Harvey, Hunt and Schroder (1961), Perry (1970) and others.

Kohlberg's data show how people reason about moral dilemma situations. He claims to have identified a culturally universal and invariant sequence of moral development comprising three levels, each subdivided into two stages. The progression is from egocentric (pre-moral, pre-conventional) thinking, through conventional role conformity to autonomous or principled judgement. Moral maturity (stages five and six) involves recognising and respecting the rights of others, acting according to conscience and principles, and taking account of other's needs and values. But few adults in fact reach the highest stages and, although one may have a characteristic stage of moral reasoning, individuals have access to a mixture of stages both above and below the dominant one.

A college study by Haan *et al.* (1968) suggested that background factors might partly account for the level of maturity reached. Only a few students in their sample reached Kohlberg's highest stage and these were largely independent of their parents, active socially and politically, and with no religious affiliations; students who operated at the level of conventional morality tended to be generally conservative, were not active socially or politically, and conformed to conventional standards set by parents and other authority figures.

Progress from level to level appears to be partly motivational and partly the need, as in logico-mathematical development, to reconcile incompatibilities perceived in 'stage mixture'. Turiel (1969) suggested that cognitive restructuring could be facilitated by presenting moral dilemmas 'one stage above' the present level of functioning; moral growth could thus be promoted if the environment provided both support and challenge to the individual.

Kohlberg and Kramer (1969) studied moral development between

16 and 24 and concluded that the major change in moral thought in the post-high school years was a significant increase in or stabilisation of conventional morality. An interesting finding was that middle class students appeared to regress in moral development between late high school and second or third year at college, and those who did not tended to be among the most mature at school. By the age of 25, however, they had returned to their earlier level, with a more tolerant outlook; Kohlberg suggests that such regression can be explained by the freedom and absence of conventional morality offered by higher education.

Harvey, Hunt and Schroder (1961) characterise conceptual systems in terms of their degree of concreteness or abstractness, and put forward a four-stage scheme in which the individual moves from unilateral dependence to interdependence. Their studies also found that high-conceptual-level individuals profit more in teaching situations where structure is low (as in independent study, and self selected projects) while low-conceptual-level students prefer concrete tasks, clearly outlined examples and no discussion. The process through the conceptual stages is not, however, clear.

Tomlinson (1974) suggests that a key factor in moral development is the growth in the individual's information processing capacity, and particularly short-term memory score. This enables the individual to take more aspects of a problem into account (open-mindedness) and also enables him to integrate information better into his existing structures. At the same time, as has been shown above, such development is not simply a part of the process of maturing: affect and motive are also clearly relevant, and the nature of the experience is also likely to be significant.

William Perry (1970) is the researcher who has related academic experience most clearly to qualitative changes in student thinking and moral development. Perry's interest in these questions stemmed from interviews conducted in the course of his work at the Bureau of Study Counsel at Harvard. He was struck by 'the variety of ways in which students responded to the relativism which permeates the intellectual and social atmosphere of a pluralistic university'. Equally he noted that students appeared to experience 'a common sequence of challenges' to which they found individual responses, which were logically ordered in the sense that the higher levels followed from and incorporated the meaning of lower levels. It is this sequence which he attempted to represent in his scheme of intellectual and ethical development and which, he claims, reflects the normal pattern of undergraduate growth.

Perry sees growth as wave-like rather than linear, a Piagetian process of assimilation and accommodation. Simple dualistic structures are gradually modified by the encounter with relativism; this process of evolution by differentiation reaches a point where revolutionary restructuring of the students' conceptual framework becomes inevitable. Relativism becomes the characteristic, integrated mode of conceiving reality. Within this framework students may move to a commitment to personal courses of action and life style which they find meaningful. This stage of 'responsibility' is seen as a development beyond Piaget's stage of formal operations.

Perry highlights the moral dilemmas and challenges which academic study presents the student. He is willed towards growth by an 'urge to mature' born of the awareness of the limitations of his existing frame of thought, and fired by the desire to emulate admired teachers and fellow students and to share their community; at the same time he is held back by a rather weaker 'urge to conserve', which both expresses itself as a 'standard' defining the optimal rate of growth the individual can cope with and mobilises old ways of thinking and learning inherited from family and community, which constitute the student's identity. The strength of this resistance means that some students 'seemed to be actively denying or fighting off within themselves awareness of their urge to progress'; they opted out by 'temporising' or marking time, 'retreating' to simpler conceptual frameworks, or 'escaping' the implications of choice, and becoming alienated. The majority, however, face up to the challenge of coping with increasing complexity and follow what Perry explicitly acknowledges to be *the* morally desirable pattern of growth for man in the contemporary world.

Perry's research spans a period of fifteen years and is based on data collected from hour-long unstructured tape-recorded interviews with 17 entrants to Harvard and Radcliffe colleges in 1954, who were followed up over the four years of their course. The scheme of development evolved from an analysis of their accounts of their experiences, and validation was subsequently attempted on a further 70 entrants in 1962 and 1973, when six postgraduate students in English and Comparative Literature, trained on a specially devised Judge's Manual, rated protocols on a global basis in terms of the scheme.

The function of interviews was to provide the student with an opportunity to interpret and to give meaning to his experience as an undergraduate. It often proved difficult to find the appropriate way into an informal discussion. In an early trial one student, when asked whether his parents would notice any difference in him, replied, after a long pause: 'Well...maybe I have put on a little weight.' Eventually students were simply invited to talk about 'whatever stands out for you about the year'; as the interview progressed specific questions on points raised by the students were put, and towards its end they might be asked to comment on aspects of their ratings on a Check List of Educational Values which they routinely filled out at the beginning and middle of each academic session.

One of the strengths of Perry's book is that he lets the students speak for themselves, selecting from the wealth of data provided in 464 transcripts. The account which follows seeks to clothe Perry's skeleton outline by illustrating in particular the development of three aspects of students' perceptions which are of greatest interest, viz. students' attitudes to knowledge, to authority (and especially their teachers) and to their own role as learners.

Perry's Developmental Scheme: Main Line of Development.

Position 1: The student sees the world in polar terms of we-right-good v. other-wrong-bad. Right Answers for everything exist in the Absolute, known to Authority whose role is to mediate (teach) them. Knowledge and goodness are perceived as quantitative accretions of discrete rightnesses to be collected by hard work and obedience (paradigm: a spelling test).

Position 2: The student perceives diversity of opinion, and uncertainty, and accounts for them as unwarranted confusion in poorly qualified Authorities or as mere exercises set by Authority 'so we can learn to find The Answer for ourselves'.

Position 3: The student accepts diversity and uncertainty as legitimate but still temporary in areas where Authority 'hasn't found The Answer yet'. He supposes Authority grades him in these areas on 'good expression' but remains puzzled as to standards.

Position 4: (a) The student perceives legitimate uncertainty (and therefore diversity of opinion) to be extensive and raises it to the status of an unstructured epistemological realm of its own in which 'anyone has a right to his own opinion', a realm which he sets over against Authority's realm where right-wrong still prevails, or (b) the student discovers qualitative contextual relativistic reasoning as a special case of 'what They want' within Authority's realm.

Figure 4.3: Perry's Scheme of Intellectual and Ethical Development

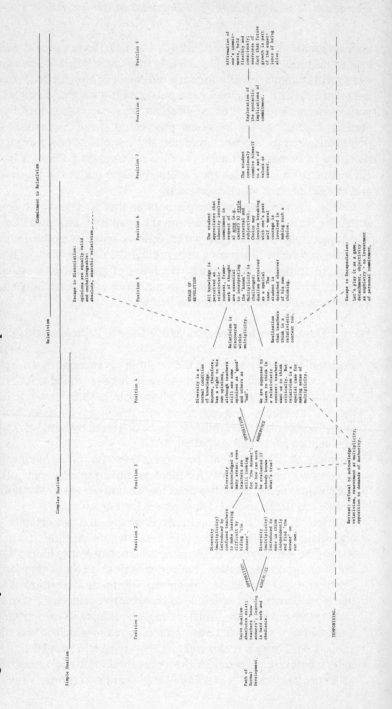

Position 5: The student perceives all knowledge and values (including Authority's) as contextual and relativistic and subordinates dualistic right-wrong functions to the status of a special case, in context.

Position 6: The student apprehends the necessity of orienting himself in a relativistic world through some form of personal Commitment (as distinct from unquestioned or unconsidered commitment to simple belief in certainty).

Position 7: The student makes an initial Commitment in some area.

Position 8: The student experiences the implications of Commitment, and explores the subjective and stylistic issues of responsibility.

Position 9: The student experiences the affirmation of identity among multiple responsibilities and realises Commitment as an ongoing, unfolding activity through which he expresses his life style. (Perry, 1970)

No student was found to hold the views expressed by Position 1: rather it is an extrapolation downwards from the frames of thinking provided by students at a higher level and from the retrospections of such students. It represents the simplest conceptualisations about knowlege, truth and the authority of the teacher: knowledge is right or wrong, truth is absolute, professors possess that truth and are to be respected, learning consists of working hard to assimilate that knowledge so that it can be given back to the professor who will reward the student for the hard work he has put into acquiring it.

When I went to my first lecture, what the man said was just like God's word, you know. I believed everything he said, because he was a professor, and he's a Harvard professor, and this was — a respected position.

But this kind of attitude is hard to maintain on a campus where the student body reflects heterogeneous intellectual and ethical values, and where the assignments and teaching force students to take account of the multiplicity of points of view on different issues. The existence of diversity or complexity is, then, quickly perceived by all as a fact of life, but in teaching and learning, Perry maintains, many students still continue to think of their studies as leading them to 'answers' which are true in respect of the field of knowledge they are studying in. They want to know, in one sentence if possible, what *really* caused the Industrial Revolution, for example. They define their teachers' role as helping them to find these 'answers', and are puzzled since most staff appear to revel in raising difficulties instead of resolving them. Perry sees two responses to this definition of the situation: combative students take the view that staff do not themselves know 'the answers'; they are ineffective and incompetent, a fit object of scorn and resentment, as the following quotation indicates:

> One comes to Harvard expecting all sorts of great things, and then one hits these, these Gen. Ed. courses which are extremely, ah, I don't know, they're just *stupid*, most of them. I've taken two,. . .both of which I found, well, it's an extremely confused sort of affair, nobody seems to know anything. . .what you get out of the course. . . is you, you get an idea that science is a terrifically confused thing in which nobody knows what's coming off anyway.

An alternative interpretation, by more submissive and conformist students, is that staff emphasise multiplicity because it is a way to teach students to think for themselves. After all, that is why you come to college. For some students this requirement to find their own 'answers' is at first disturbing:

> that's something I never had to do, think things out by myself, I mean. In high school two and two was four; there's nothing to think out there. In here they try to make your mind work, and I didn't realise that last year until the end of the year.

But the experience of 'standing on your own feet' is maturing, and ultimately welcomed by most students:

> it's a more mature way of teaching. It puts responsibility on your own shoulders. . .At first it scared me, and. . .it seemed like you were in a shooting gallery. And they were shooting at you. As I say,

it's more of a mature way of teaching, and ah-huh. . .I think it teaches a person to become dependent upon himself, more than it would in high school, where somebody's holding a whip over your head, and sending you down to the office if you don't do anything right.

If Position 2 reflects an opening of the student mind to the existence of multiplicity, all learning is still conceived of as a process of finding answers which staff have tucked up their sleeves or mislaid in their cleverness. In Position 3, however, the student has come to accept that there are no 'answers' to many issues, at least in our present state of knowledge. That is the justification for research: 'in physics you get definite answers to a point. Beyond that point you know there *are* definite answers, but you can't reach them'. A 'yet' is implied here. But it dawns on the student that many of the exercises he is set are open-ended: how, if there are no 'right answers', can staff discriminate between the opinions of different students? What kind of answers do 'They' want? At school hard work was recognised and rewarded: 'the teacher could tell whether you were working hard, and he would give you breaks if he knew you were working. It wasn't grading a student on his aptitude, it was grading someone on the amount of work he put in'. But at college it is quality not quantity that counts: students who put in what seemed a minimum of work often received better grades than those who slogged for hours.

Perry suggests that, again, students adopt one of two stances in response to this new perception of reality. The awareness of relativism leads some students to adopt a combative, oppositional interpretation of multiplicity. Since everyone is entitled to a view on an issue, no opinion can be perceived as better or worse than another — all opinions are equal. The student can find support for his view from the academic world itself: 'I mean if you read them [critics], that's the great thing about a book like *Moby Dick*. (Laughs) *Nobody* understands it.' The student is justified in putting forward his own opinions on the book, but displays ignorance of the frameworks within which interpretations of literature derive their significance. While assuming the right to his own opinions he implies that in academic debate consensus is an important aspect of truth. Within multiplicity he makes dualistic categorisation the characteristic feature of his teacher's world.

The alternative, conformist approach within Position 4 reflects student learning of 'the way they want you to think' about issues. Staff emphasise relativism, comparing viewpoints, examining assumptions;

students adopt this style first of all for extrinsic reasons, particularly grades, but also because they find the experience a satisfying and liberating one. But the experience is also testing since students may lack confidence in their ability to criticise authorities:

> I'll read the topic for a paper and then I'll choose a side, or choose a point — and another thing, I'm not as scared to, to differ with them and say 'Well I don't think so'. Ah, I think the courage comes with sections. I think it's easier to disagree in sections than it is when a lecturer is saying such and such from his podium. In sections we have differences of opinion and there are arguments on one side and the other, and you see the section man himself sometimes changing his opinion and this is encouraging.

The changes so far described have reflected the gradual assimilation of relativistic frameworks to a world view which is basically dualistic: the evolution of thinking has resulted in the loosening and modifying of the old structure, but at Position 5 the evolutionary process is overtaken by a revolutionary restructuring of the definition of the nature of knowledge: all knowing is perceived as relativistic and the dualistic view is relegated to the status of a special case. The process of evolution leading to revolution is like that of the chick maturing in the egg: it can develop so far within the environment of the shell, but there comes a point at which it has to redefine the scope of its environment — it breaks the shell and embraces a new world. There is a parallel, too, in Kuhn's (1962) account of the structure of scientific revolutions: awareness of the limited explanations provided by current paradigms leads to a search for alternative theories to explain discrepancies between existing theory and knowledge — a reinterpretation of the data in terms of a Copernican revolution provides a more complete and satisfying explanation which can subsequently be tested empirically.

The student perceives the relativism of knowledge: context and frame of thought are essential for knowing. The role of the learner is to get to grips with the assumptions underlying ideas:

> *Then*, it was just the weight of the thing. *Now*, it's not so much how many pages there are on the reading list, it's more what the books are worth. What sort of ideas do they have. I mean, I'm looking for the ideas rather than plodding over the words. . . I mean, before maybe I was reading, whereas *now* I tend to generalise the thing

and get the main ideas and concepts, and then pick up a few illustrations here and there...

The legitimacy of staff authority is seen to reside in their greater experience and sophistication in exploring issues which the student himself is confronting: staff are perceived as 'human', people with whom you can discuss things and from whom advice can be sought on problems. The lack of pressure by staff on such matters as attendance, on submitting assignments on time, meant that combative students found it easy to slip out of that role and find a *modus vivendi* with staff.

Another feature of this position is the capacity for detachment: the student becomes conscious that he can perceive different situations or problems from different points of view. He is able to think about the way he thinks:

> The more I work here, the more I feel that what I'm trying to do is — ah become what you might call a detached observer of various situations, of any type of situation that you go into. And by that I mean — ah, one who can, to the utmost of his ability, detach himself — ah emotionally from the problems and look at the various sides of the problem in an objective, empirical type of way — look at the pros and cons of a situation and then try to. . .analyse and formulate a, a judgement — a value judgement it could be on your part. . .bringing into consideration in this judgement — ah, well, what the other person would feel and why he would feel so. I think it all boils down to trying to remove emotionalism from your decisions and from your life as much as possible. . . It's just a matter of whether such a method of learning can go on working anyway. . . can be transferred from the college atmosphere to. . .to. . .everyday work situations.

Detachment may be a preliminary to action, or it may become an end in itself, a self-indulgent balancing of arguments which serves as an excuse for inactivity. The student above shows awareness that his new found mastery of thinking, and his own thinking, have relevance for issues in the real world. He is looking beyond Position 5 towards commitment. Perry describes the completed Position 5 as 'Relativism Diffuse' — the latter term because of its 'connotation of vagueness or lack of focus, for it is just this quality that distinguishes this structure from the developments which are to follow'. The instability and lack of orientation of the position gives it a key role for the educator who seeks to promote 'commitment' in his students; the alternative is into 'escape' and alienation.

The thinking associated with Position 5, then, reflects movement to a plane that is qualitatively different from that which preceded it: no student who had once accepted a relativistic epistemology *as context* showed evidence of abandoning that position.

The remainder of Perry's scheme is devoted to mapping out the growth of the student's sense of commitment to himself as a maker of meaning in his personal life. Personal identity derives from both the content and the forms or stylistic aspects of commitments. Values are both expressed in and derived from the choice of field of study, career, marriage, etc., but the way one plays the role is as significant as the role itself. Perry distinguishes between such 'external' factors as emphasis between, for example, studies and extra-curricular activities, or number versus intensity of friendships, and 'subjective' balances such as those between action and contemplation, or permanence and flexibility.

In Position 6 the student shows that he is aware of the need to define himself both in terms of area and style; in Position 7 a commitment has been entered into — values or a career or area of specialisation have been accepted; in Position 8 the student shows that he is conscious that the way he acts within the role is as important as the role itself; Position 9 'describes a maturity in which a person has developed an experience of "who he is" in his commitments both in their content and in his style of living them'. An aspect of that maturity involves awareness that life itself is a constant process of self-definition and re-affirmation.

Alternatives to Growth. As mentioned above growth is neither linear nor continuous. The process is one of coming to terms with complexity and students differ in their capacity to cope with the intellectual and emotional stresses which are involved. As one student remarked — 'a guy could really go to pieces around here'.

The alternatives to growth are Temporising, Retreat and Escape. Temporising, defined as a pause in growth over one full academic year, is most vivid in Position 6 where the student is conscious of the need to make a commitment, but waits for experience or ageing to take him to the point of decision. Clearly 'marking time' may merge insidiously into 'drifting' or responding opportunistically to events. Retreat is rare: it refers specifically 'to an entrenchment in the dualism of Position 2 or 3 — an entrenchment undertaken in reaction to the complexities, envisioned or experienced, of more advanced positions'. Essentially it is a retreat from awareness of relativism (Position 4) rather than from higher positions. It involves dramatic and energetic defence of a dualistic perception in a pluralistic context; Perry equates such a position with paranoia. The student turns against the college, the staff, the assignments — and even learning itself:

> This place is full of bull. They don't want anything really honest from you. If you turn in something, a speech that's well written, whether it's got one single fact in it or not is beside the point. That's sort of annoying at times, too. You can put things over on people around here; you're almost given to try somehow to sit down and write a paper in an hour, just because you know that whatever it is isn't going to make any difference to anybody. If you make one good point in a paper, one ten word sentence, somebody will think it's very nice, and that's so silly, really, because it's completely meaningless.
>
> You know, I said I didn't like all this bull around here. On the other hand, I don't really — scholarship doesn't appeal to me, sitting in the library stocks, peering at birds and things like that outside. It makes no sense to me either. I think it's nice to know things and have the feeling when you do know it that you never learned it. I hate the feeling of learning something.

Escape involves denial of self and is a form of alienation. Fromm (1955) defines the alienated person as someone

> estranged from himself. He does not experience himself as the centre of his world, as the creator of his own acts — but his acts and their consequences have become his masters whom he obeys or whom he may even worship. The alienated person is out of touch with himself as he is out of touch with any other person.

One part of this notion corresponds to escape 'Toward dissociation' or 'passive delegation of all responsibility to fate': since every opinion can be justified there is no need to assert personal meaning. Another aspect is escape 'toward encapsulation' where the student embraces the game of relativism and manipulates the forms of knowing, but invests none of his own energies.

Finally, 'escape may be a blind rush into commitment for the sake of being committed'.

> You have to get out and, and do something, make some, take some stand. Certainly that's a necessary part. You have to, of course, that may be just the choice; *between* stands again, the various stands that you can take.

This kind of escape from complexity, the fear of freedom which Fromm (1942) highlighted as the flight from democratic responsibility into authoritarianism, is a widespread phenomenon. Perry (1977) suggests that its growth may be intensified if the naive hope implicit in dualistic thinking is challenged too early in life: primary and nursery schools which teach relativistic thinking run the risk of offering children bandwagons which may be climbed on too easily and which, by seeking to promote 'sophisticated' thinking, undermine the basis on which it may develop.

Comments on Perry's Scheme. Perry presents the general developmental path of students from the students' own viewpoint. The modal position of first year students has risen steadily — from Positions 3/4 in June 1954 to Position 5 in 1959. Writing in 1974 Perry speculated that most entering students were probably beyond Position 5: 'they may not be well-versed in the disciplines of contextual contingent thinking, but they are familiar with diversity and already take it for granted that "this is how things are"' (Perry, 1977).

But these positionings are based on global ratings: ratings produced for different aspects of the students' development (academic, extracurricular, interpersonal, vocational, religious) 'revealed a considerable disparity in the students' development from sector to sector, especially in his outlook toward academic work and religion as compared to his outlook toward his career'. Laurillard (1978) at the University of Surrey has found a similar discrepancy. All 30 students she worked with, irrespective of year of course, 'expressed implicit theories of knowledge which were relativistic', but she did report a sequence of development like Perry's in students' relationships to staff and in taking responsibility for their own progress as learners.

With all the wealth of data at his command Perry's reporting is disappointingly unsystematic. He does not relate global position to academic performance nor, as Entwistle (1977) has observed, does he consider whether the subject matter of science and arts is equally effective in inducing awareness of relativism, or whether brighter students proceed more rapidly through the Positions than average students.

His main contribution lies in the framework of his scheme and in highlighting the nature of the radical transformation in the process of thinking which the student is required to undergo if he is to master the learning tasks set in higher education. In the light of the greater intellectual maturity of entrants to higher education Perry appears to exaggerate the gap between school and university teaching, but if the contrast is not between 'dualism' and 'relativism' it is certain that in higher education the student will be set to extend and deepen his conception of understanding. Student performance in tutorials, the laboratory and the lecture and in essays, examinations and projects will reflect assumptions about the nature of knowledge, the purpose of learning and appropriate teacher-student relationships. Teachers must act towards students aware of 'where the learner is'.

Assuming that 'growth' in Perry's terms is held to be desirable, what are the conditions for promoting it? The basic need would appear to be to provide an environment which offers support and challenge to students. Widick and Simpson (1978) have attempted to design such teaching programmes in the humanities and psychology and claim some measure of success in promoting growth through the stages. Knefelkamp and Slepitza (1978) have also used Perry's work as the basis of a career decision-making model.

Perry himself sees implications for selection, counselling and teaching. An intellectually and socially heterogeneous student community is an important factor in making students aware of alternatives to their established ways of thinking. Counselling both signifies a personal concern for the student and, if structured along the lines of interviews conducted for the investigation, forces the student to articulate and hence recognise his dilemmas. In teaching, staff model the intellectual skills they wish students to acquire; equally, in the way they handle assessments they can help students understand the nature of the intellectual development they are expected to demonstrate. Assignments reflect students' attempts to make meaning and assessment should be undertaken in an awareness of the significance of that achievement. A piece of work may represent the fruits of a personal struggle to reach a more sophisticated level of understanding: alternatively it may be a ritualistic exercise devoid of personal commitment. Assessment directed at the individual as well as at the quality of the work may be a means to confirmation in a more sophisticated level of thinking: alternatively it may be designed to promote dissatisfaction and to reinforce the urge to grow.

The diagnostic evaluation Perry is recommending is time consuming and few staff have the opportunity to assess or the continuity of contact with first year students which would be necessary for building up the detailed personal picture which Perry regards as desirable. In most cases assessment will be at a distance and impersonal, although it may be hoped that it will be constructive (Rowntree, 1977) rather than antagonistic.

Perry's work, then, raises many questions about the nature of student growth and the direction of its development. There is considerable scope for investigating the generalisability of his findings and for quantifying the rather impressionistic picture he presents.

(b) A Dimensional Model of Development

A stage model of growth and development in childhood and adolescence is currently controversial (e.g. Brown and Desforges, 1977 and 1979; Shayer, 1979). Hunt (1978) has had second thoughts about its usefulness for describing the process of learning in higher education. Stage theorists, he maintains, define each stage's characteristics as much on logico-deductive principles as on empirical evidence and then define the 'transition rules' for growth, essentially the environmental characteristics of support and challenge which enable the student to 'move forward' from his present 'deficit' position to the higher stage. Evidence for the existence of stages comes from performance measures and qualitative interpretations of students' accounts of their thinking processes, but since both the nature of the stages and the sequence of progression are already defined on logical grounds the self-fulfilling nature of such schemes becomes apparent — only evidence which 'fits' the stages is judged to be valid and contrary evidence is discarded. Moreover stage theory is unhelpful in a practical sense. High level theories are simply 'metaphors for practitioners who work in the world of specific persons, times and places'. Growth involves understanding the complete person — his identity, intentions, present base of knowledge, competence and actions. Thus Hunt focuses attention on the context of teaching and learning and on theories which highlight interactions between the learner's perception and the teacher's ability to 'read' and 'flex' to the situation. Similar reservations are expressed by Widick and Simpson (1978) in evaluating their attempt to promote progress through Perry's development stages.

Peck and Havighurst (1960) and Douglas Heath (1978) also

challenge the view that development involves qualitative discontinuities and maintain that growth is continuous, if uneven, and that differences over time are quantitative rather than qualitative. On this view the adult is occupied with the same conflicts as the adolescent — over identity, relationships with others, security, etc. — but the generations differ simply in life experience, which means that older people generally have greater capacity to cope with such problems and more resources (e.g. financial) to resolve them. Peck and Havighurst (1960) found that over the years 10 to 16 adolescents remained within the same 'stage' of moral development, relative to their peers, although naturally how they manifested moral behaviour changed considerably.

The entire age group develops and changes through the years, but each individual child tends to maintain about the same generalised attitudes, and also the same standing relative to the total population, in terms of the quality and age-appropriate maturity of his character structure and moral behaviour.

Heath (1978) emphasises that an adequate model of student development must take account of the growth of the total personality, and not simply cognitive aspects. He suggests that 'maturity' is a product of neurophysiological change, as at puberty, encounter with new and challenging environments (such as entering higher education), and acceptance of personal challenge with the reappraisal of life style that involves. His dimensions of maturity (see Figure 4.4) emerged from a content analysis of the attributes of the liberally educated man,

Figure 4.4: D. Heath's (1978) Model of Maturing

Dimensions of maturity

Psychological dimensions	Symbolisation	Allocentricism	Integration	Stability	Autonomy
Cognitive skills					
Self-concept					
Values					
Inter-personal relations					

as defined by educational philosophers, and the psychological dimensions are those relevant for personal functioning (Heath, 1965). Thus as one gets older cognitive skills, for example, become increasingly articulated (symbolisation), analytic, judgemental and logical (allocentric), differentiated and relational (integration), stabilised and resilient (stable) and mobile and transferable (autonomy).

Growth on this universal model is systemic in that development along one dimension can only proceed so far until other aspects 'catch up'. Studies of students suggest that growth is neither linear nor continuous but rather proceeds in fits and starts, often after lengthy periods of inactivity.

Heath suggests that entering students may experience confusion and uncertainty about their role and this will result in attempts to articulate feelings (symbolisation), which in turn will reflect values and self-concept. The more mature person will have more complex and differentiated value systems and will be better able to articulate them. More mature students' self-ratings of their personal traits agree closely with the ratings provided by friends and colleagues and this is suggestive of greater self-insight. Mature students are also better able to organise themselves and they are more determined and more emotionally stable than immature students.

Heath suggests that institutions differ markedly in the extent to which they promote different aspects of maturity with some, for example, being more effective than others in promoting allocentricism. By 'allocentricism' he means the capacity to relate to others, to communicate, and the development of social conscience. Mature students have a greater capacity to empathise which implies a more differentiated perception of reality and consequently increased integration of outlook. Effective integration will produce stability, which is reminiscent of the psychoanalytic concept of ego–strength, i.e. the capacity of more mature minds to tolerate and cope with more threatening kinds of ideas (e.g. sexual or political) without being overwhelmed by the emotions which they arouse and which threaten to sweep away rational response. Finally, maturity implies developing autonomy both in the sense of responding discriminatingly to environmental pressures (e.g. the demands of new learning tasks), and in controlling one's impulses and wishes. Heath suggests that autonomy is illustrated in application of acquired learning skills in 'new' situations, but the autonomous person is also more in control of his self-concept and has more stable and personally-held values. While acknowledging the considerable body of research still required to develop knowledge of the process of maturing, Heath argues that his scheme throws up hypotheses and interrelationships between variables in a way which 'stage theory' does not, and it is accordingly likely to prove a more fruitful approach for understanding the process of student development.

It is possible to see parallels between Heath's model and the 'modal' view of change put forward by writers such as Chickering (1969) who describes student development in terms of (1) achieving competence (intellectual, physical, social and interpersonal) and a sense of competence; (2) managing emotions (especially sexual and aggressive emotions) and interpreting others' emotions correctly; (3) developing autonomy and emotional independence of others; (4) establishing a sense of identity, including an awareness of one's strengths and weaknesses; (5) freeing interpersonal relations, i.e. developing tolerance and seeing people in their own right; (6) clarifying purposes, especially vocational plans and recreational interests; and (7) developing integrity, i.e. a personally valid set of beliefs. Such dimensions have, for the most part, been assessed by means of attitude questionnaires and some of these changes have been identified.

Patterns of Student Development: A Synthesis

The discussion so far has contrasted a conception of student development in terms of progression through a series of discrete intellectual stages with one which has emphasised the different and interacting aspects of growth towards maturity at a particular point in time. How opposed in reality are these two versions of student development?

Hunt and Sullivan (1974) clarify the issue by distinguishing between the different perspectives from which growth may be perceived. Stage theory sees present behaviour in terms of the development of the individual over his life span, and enables explanations to be advanced in terms of past experience and present 'stage' or 'level'. It is important for the teacher to have this wider perspective as a guide in planning a curriculum which will offer the learner the necessary support and challenge to take him beyond his present level of functioning.

Equally, however, in face-to-face encounters teachers assess students according to how they strike them and this may be as 'types' — the dependent, the articulate, or the self-confident — reflecting their behaviour on Douglas Heath's (1978) dimensions of maturity. It is easier to think of individuals from a 'type' perspective than from a 'developmental' perspective: we operate on stereotypes in social encounters.

Stage theory emphasises change and development: there is an implication that 'types' are static and fixed. The truth may be that certain aspects of the individual are relatively unchanging while others are susceptible to quite radical changes. Peck and Havighurst's (1960) findings on moral development have already been mentioned; temperament, too, may be relatively fixed. Both moral level and temperament may reflect inherited characteristics and the formative experiences of early upbringing and parental modelling. Physiological effects can cause changes in temperament, of course: liver disease induces depression and barbiturates help tense and anxious people to relax. Situations make different demands on people, but experience suggests that they react in predictable ways, showing that temperament is relatively consistent over time. Cognitive abilities, on the other hand, do appear to change qualitatively between early childhood and adolescence, and this may reflect both interaction with the environment and the process of maturing. Attitudes and level of motivation appear to be highly susceptible to manipulation: behaviouristic psychology emphasises how positive feedback promotes the desire to learn, and Bloom (1976) has shown how mastery learning techniques can change pupils' attitudes towards their work. These artificially induced changes in affect can become functionally autonomous (Allport, 1937) in that students become 'hooked' to study, with striking increases in level of academic achievement. Depending on the aspects of the individual we focus on, it is possible that students are recognisably the 'same' at the end of their course and yet also unmistakably different.

An interesting longitudinal study of 36 randomly selected students, matched with controls, carried out by Roy Heath (1964 and 1978), a clinical psychologist, at Princeton in 1954 provides some relevant evidence. Students were interviewed at the beginning and end of each session, and informal observational data were also obtained to enable ratings to be made on intellectual development, personality, satisfaction with academic work, friendship with peers, self-understanding and acceptance.

Heath rated students on temperament and maturity, initially on the basis of how they handled themselves in interview. Temperament appeared a fixed characteristic, but many students moved towards increased maturity over their time at university, and Heath groups them into various 'types' on the basis of their attitudes in the interview.

Figure 4.5 describes Roy Heath's model of development. At the 'withdrawn' end of the continuum of temperament were non-committers (X) who volunteered little information about themselves, replying monosyllabically that things were 'fine'. At the 'hyperactive' end plungers (Z) tended to take over the interview. Unpredictable of mood, which might be sullen and depressed or effervescent, these students found the interview cathartic and they would jump from topic to topic in a rambling, free-association style. Between these extremes 'hustlers' (Y) accepted the interviewers' definition of the situation, but sought to present themselves in the best possible light. Thus they anticipated the questions they would be asked so that their answers would come 'pat'; generally, too, they displayed activist, competitive, tough and assertive attitudes. These diverse reactions were manifest in everyday behaviour. Hustlers, like cue seekers, would raise points with the tutor at the end of the class. They also displayed a more realistic self-evaluation of their examination performance than plungers, who were usually pessimistic, or non-committers, whose complacency led them to overestimate their actual success.

Figure 4.5: Model of Dimensions of Student Development (R. Heath, 1964)

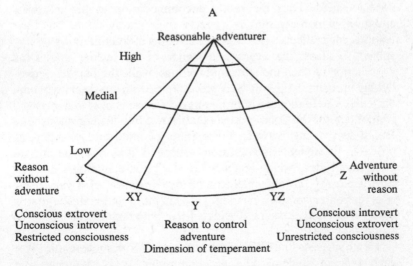

'Reasonable adventurers' are Heath's ideal, mature students with outstanding intellectual gifts. They are rational, confident and assured, enjoying the opportunity to play with ideas, and with a capacity for detachment both from themselves and from the student scene at Princeton. They made many close friendships and were notable for their tolerance of ambiguity, independence of mind, breadth of interests and sense of humour. They played a leading role on the campus. Each type of student was capable of developing towards this ideal, but only 7 of the sample were thus categorised in first year and even by fourth the number had risen only to 16 (45 per cent). Heath is conscious that within the student body as a whole this may be an over-estimate since participation in the study in itself constituted a maturing influence.

Heath argues, like the stage theorists, that each type of student is coping with different 'deficit needs' and consequently requires differential educational and counselling experience to move upwards. His clinical background leads him to postulate an explanation in terms of style of ego functioning or 'the manner in which the self interacts with the world, achieves its satisfaction, and defends itself (or fails to defend itself) from threats to its survival, both external and internal'. Drawing on Jungian theory, he postulates that overt manifestation of one trait (e.g. extraversion) is compensated by covert manifestation of its opposite (i.e. introversion) (Heath, 1978). Moreover temperament may reflect the efficiency with which the brain or mind filters out consciousness. Thus the ready accommodation to the interview situation of non-committers reflects their extraversion, but their complacency reflects a repression or levelling of potentially disturbing, subjective ideas; the aggressive stance of the hustler marks the suppression of alien thoughts and feelings, while the plunger, super-ficially introvert in the way he is preoccupied with imaginary personal difficulties and fantasies of impending disaster, is overwhelmed and cannot control the flood of ideas that crowd into his consciousness. Heath sees a link between these traits of mind and the thinking process. Reasonable adventurers 'suspend action to permit an interplay of ideas which leads to novelty'; non-committers are 'left with a paucity, an enfeeblement of ideas because of a very early intervention of control'; hustlers get 'caught in ambivalence that is unresolved', and plungers 'dissipate ideas with their disinclination to suspend action'.

Heath suggests that different experiences will promote maturity for each type of student. The non-committer needs challenge and stimulation (e.g. through literature), both in the counselling situation and in tutorial, where his complacency must be shaken and he must come to feel that his contribution is valuable in itself. Dramatic failure forces the hustler to examine his attitude to study: he needs group therapy to help him understand the effect he has on people: his pseudo-self must be exposed for the front it is so that he can come to terms with himself. The plunger needs both an audience, and acceptance for its own sake: but equally he must be helped towards self-discipline and coherent expression of his thoughts and ideas.

David Reisman refers somewhat disparagingly to Princeton as a 'stag school' where even the final year students 'talk in clichés' and have 'little sense of ideas', but by final year three-quarters of Heath's sample seemed to have found intrinsic interest in their academic work. Heath suggests that the curriculum, especially in humanities, and the senior thesis played a key role in the development of student thinking. But residence, and close friendships in a peer group where students 'inspired' each other, were also held to be important factors.

Conclusion

Astin's model, with which the chapter began, suggests the framework within which research on the 'effects' of college on the intellectual and moral development of students might be conducted. It is self-evident to most staff that colleges do have effects on their students, but 'impact' studies, with their 'before' and 'after' approach and crude criteria of benefit, have clarified neither the nature nor the magnitude of the changes, nor, more importantly, have they pinpointed the factors which facilitate the desired types of growth.

At the end of the last chapter it was suggested that students simply learn a cynical conformity to the demands of the course: Musgrove (1964) echoed this, and approvingly endorsed Michael Young's observation that our modern undergraduates are in danger of becoming cautious old men at twenty. But many students are also idealists seeking in late adolescence a purpose and commitment in life, and the studies of Perry and Heath provide a corrective by showing how the academic subject, and the context of the university, can provide the support and challenge which may result in a qualitative change in intellectual functioning and a more sensitive moral outlook.

In many ways the perspectives adopted by these two researchers are complementary. Perry identifies different routes towards maturity, while Heath describes different types of student; the two may simply be different ways of representing the same phenomena from different standpoints. Both identify some outstanding students (rather like the cue seekers) who command the respect and admiration of the researchers: one significant factor is that many 'reasonable adventurers' and 'committed' students appear to have developed their intellectual and moral qualities even before they came to university. Yet the experience of academic study is not without its importance: it channels and focuses their qualities and provides a content through which they are expressed.

The most common shift in outlook that Perry describes is from Position 5, which represents the typical entry state of an increasing proportion of students, towards commitment. Experience with honours level students suggests that such commitment to the subject is essential if students are to maintain interest over a course, and the importance many students attach to academic study is reflected in the high proportion who seek careers which will enable them to maintain contact with their discipline. But the evidence of *décalage* provided by Perry himself, and confirmed by Laurillard (1978), suggests that other aspects of student development (such as accepting personal responsibility for one's own progress) may not be so far 'advanced': student development appears to be uneven and to reflect temperament and personality. Heath's 'hustlers', for example, who are critical of staff, appear to move forward through a path similar to that described as 'opposition', while non-committers appear to be more prepared to give 'adherence' to the lead staff offer. But much fuller mapping out of the content of these different positions is required, in relation to the different dimensions of development and individual differences between students.

The limitations of these studies are rather apparent. Both were conducted in elite institutions in the United States; performance data are lacking; and the claims made for the effects of social context and curricular experiences are general rather than specific. It is to these issues that attention is directed in the chapters which follow. The next chapter looks specifically at the evidence of the effect of the peer group on student development, while subsequent chapters focus on how students tackle particular learning tasks.

5   LEARNING FROM OTHER STUDENTS

Encounter with contemporaries from different backgrounds, specialisms and values can, according to Perry (1970) and Roy Heath (1964), lead to challenge, self-questioning and informal learning which promotes the moral and intellectual development of students. Indeed, one powerful criticism of policies of 'goodness of fit' (e.g. Stern, 1970) in higher education is that opportunities for growth might be restricted if student and institutional characteristics were matched too closely. It is certainly the case that most students learn in the company of fellow students or the peer group. But it is not so clear what role the peer group plays in student learning, or the implications of differences in the composition of the peer group in different institutions. It is to these questions that we turn in this chapter.

Composition and Role of the Peer Group

College peer groups will differ in composition from institution to institution, and even from department to department. Academic selectivity and reputation, the function of the institution and the subjects which may be studied, religious affiliation, size, setting (urban or rural), antiquity and traditions — these and many other factors will be reflected in the ability, sex balance and social class characteristics of the students. Students, too, are likely to be differentially exposed to the influence of the peer group. The status and personality of the individual, and social factors such as residence, will be important determinants of effects. Participation may reflect need and willingness to seek out social contacts: some students are 'loners' who resist attempts to involve them; others form a firm friendship with a member of the same or opposite sex, and may find that relationship adequate for their social and emotional needs. Some are married, and their family commitments off the campus limit their contacts. A few are likely to be prominent in student activities and may serve as influential 'models' to less able or more insecure students. Students may belong to different 'sets' whose *raison d'être* is the dramatic society or the SRC or sport. Social life can be so stimulating for some that academic work becomes an interference!

One way of thinking about the peer group is in terms of the functions it may fulfil for students. Essentially there are three: it provides a means of learning, it supports students emotionally in coping with the pressures of academic work, and it provides a means to fulfilment of personal needs and social status.

Learning through the peer group may be planned for by staff, or it may occur incidentally; it may relate to the formal curriculum (the course the student is taking), or to the informal curriculum (those aspects of general personal development which higher education is said to promote) (see Figure 5.1).

Figure 5.1: Peer Group Effects on Learning in Higher Education

		Learning in the peer group	
		incidental	planned by staff
Curriculum of higher education	formal (course of study)	1 e.g. discussion of course work, assignments out of class	2 e.g. peer teaching; leaderless discussion methods
	informal (general personal development)	3 e.g. discussion of moral/social issues	4 e.g. projects, reading parties

Formal learning may occur incidentally (cell 1) when students discuss their work together out of class. In some cases, of course, discussion can lead to collaboration or even straightforward cribbing. But staff can also engineer student learning (cell 2) by exploiting possibilities of students teaching each other (peer teaching), and by the deliberate use of teaching methods such as project and leaderless discussion situations. The use of such methods often produces social cohesion which may lead to opportunities for learning in the informal curriculum (cell 4). Finally, learning in the informal curriculum may occur incidentally (cell 3) when topical issues are discussed in what the Americans would describe as 'bull sessions', or commonroom debates; students often draw upon ideas from their reading or courses in such situations, and may deliberately model their behaviour on the style of admired teachers or fellow students. Another aspect of informal learning occurs in relation to attitudes and aspirations: rubbing shoulders with students with high or low commitment may influence the level of award the student himself aims for.

The peer group also has an important supportive role. Students in a class are, like Marx's proletariat, faced with a common predicament. They can support each other in coping with the pressures of the workload and in escaping from it, perhaps to the pub. Fellow students, and especially those in senior years, constitute a reference group which may encourage the individual to persevere, and from which he derives social support. They can also provide, through the 'grapevine', practical advice as to which courses or options to choose.

Finally, the peer group provides a means to fulfilment of personal needs and social status. It is important to remember that students are developing socially, sexually and emotionally through their years in higher education; their definition of a 'successful term' is likely to be broader than the academic's. Our more prominent lawyers and politicians are largely self-trained via the informal curriculum of debates in college unions. Journalism and the West End have been the beneficiaries of a stream of talent which has served its apprenticeship editing student newspapers or starring with the Cambridge Footlights. Recent revelations suggest that a latent function of higher education is for recruiting spies and homosexuals. Friendships and liaisons provide many students with personal fulfilment: higher education is a marriage bureau as well as an academic marketplace. Indeed, many students may see a rugby blue, stardom in the student revue, or winning the *Observer* Mace as being of greater significance than the 'glittering prizes' of conventional academic success.

Staff-directed Peer Group Learning

Many staff would regard it as desirable to promote student involvement in academic work outside the normal meetings of the class. One way of doing so is by 'peer tutoring'. Goldschmid and Goldschmid (1976) suggest that this may involve two roles: senior students may help 'freshers' to cope with new subject matter, or to settle down at college; alternatively, students of equal status may 'teach' each other through, for example, leaderless group discussions (e.g. Rudduck, 1978) or learning cells consisting of 'dyads' where students alternate the roles of teacher and taught.

Although much of the evidence is impressionistic, it appears that peer tutoring confers important cognitive and affective benefits on students. The teaching role forces the student to 'learn how to learn' to consolidate his grasp of the subject, but his need for guidance on teaching points brings him closer to the senior staff; in addition to learning how to structure materials the student is obliged to become an assessor and general consultant too. Peer teaching also benefits the recipient: he appears to learn as much as under conventional instruction, but to remember it better, and to develop more highly his capacity for creative thinking and problem solving. Although the success of peer tutoring depends on effective selection and matching of students and tutors, as well as the preparation of carefully structured materials, the change from a competitive to a co-operative model of learning does appear to engender more positive attitudes. Project methods, though not without their weaknesses and difficulties (e.g. Adderley *et al.*, 1975), appear to have similar effects.

Peer group learning is to be seen as a supplement to, rather than as a replacement for, traditional teaching approaches. The Goldschmids suggest that the method is most relevant 'when one seeks to maximise the student's responsibility for his own learning, and active participation in the learning process, and to enhance the development of skills for co-operation and social interaction'.

It is perhaps rather obvious that teaching methods can affect staff-student relationships: what is not always appreciated is that their effect on the ethos of a department can influence students' attitudes to each other and to their work. Rutter *et al.* (1979) have defined 'ethos' as 'the climate of expectations and modes of behaving' of staff and students in an institution. One study which illustrated the importance of ethos for student learning was carried out by Parlett and King (1971) at the Massachusetts Institute of Technology. The typical student experience at MIT has been fully documented by Snyder (1971): the institution is competitive, there is little group identity, and no co-operation outside of class. As one student put it: 'one is throughout the term effectively a stranger to 70-90 per cent of the students'. All this was changed for one group of twenty students by the introduction of a course of 'concentrated study' in place of the regular programme. This required students to undertake full-time study of a single subject for a short period, with no concurrent academic commitments. The professor in charge, John King, an outstanding lecturer in physics, was able to infect his students with his own enthusiasm for the subject and this had a marked effect not only on staff-student relationships, but also on peer group interaction. Nine of the students claimed that the amount they had learned from the course was related to the fact that they had become personally involved with the subject matter through the lecturer. Identification with the other members of the class led to more work being done, more problems being discussed out of class, and the development of more relaxed attitudes to work. One student summed this up by saying that he felt he could ask 'dumber questions'.

Of course any teaching which is 'different' creates its own Hawthorne effect. Students welcome opportunities for sustained interaction with staff in small group situations; they enjoy the opportunities for playing a more independent role which discussions, projects and reading parties provide. The teacher-student relationship is more equal: learning involves 'sharing' knowledge and perceptions, and discovering weaknesses as well as strengths. The problem for staff is the time demands of such methods, and this in turn raises the question of the priority to be accorded teaching as compared to activities such as research and consultancy.

The Nature and Role of the Peer Group in Different Institutions

Institutions of higher education in Britain and the United States differ strikingly in selectivity. Entwistle *et al.* (1971) found a clear pecking order in terms of school qualifications of students in universities, polytechnics and the now almost vanished college of education sector in England. Watts (1972) has confirmed the elite recruitment pattern to Oxbridge. Students are attracted to the most prestigious colleges because of the quality of the staff and the status of the awards; staff because of the quality of the students and the research facilities. It might be expected that the selective nature of the peer group would in itself be an important source of stimulus to high academic achievement. On the other hand, the competition experienced in such a situation might have negative effects on students who have difficulty in excelling. The literature provides support for both of these interpretations.

Several studies by Astin (e.g. 1972 and 1973) have found that selective institutions in the United States do give more good degrees than non-selective institutions. On the other hand, the ratio is smaller than expected in the light of the striking difference in calibre of the intakes. Staff simply mark 'on the curve', on a norm-referenced model, whatever the quality of the students. 'Low performers' in selective institutions are, in fact, as able as high performers in non-selective colleges. Selective colleges appear to have too many 'big frogs in a small pond' for the staff to cope with: they make fine (and unreliable) distinctions between them in terms of what are in fact uniformly high academic performances. It is not surprising therefore, that the self-image of these 'low' achievers is poorer than in less selective colleges. Indeed, it has been suggested that this 'shock' experience of relative failure will lower the students' expectations and increase the probability of drop-out. Mental illness, too, may be one of the costs of failure (Snyder, 1971), and may lead to higher suicide rates. Parnell's (1951) finding that suicide at Oxford was eleven times that of the general population of comparable age would fit in with this view, as would the findings of Malleson (1963) and other researchers that students as a group are little different from the general population in terms of psychiatric breakdown.

Tinto (1975), however, has suggested that students are aware of the relative prestige of different institutions, and even those of relatively low academic ability will stay on at an elite college to get their degree. The American evidence certainly appears to support this interpretation: selective colleges, measured both by the ability of the intake and the number of PhDs on the staff, retain poorer performers more than might be expected. The chances of a student of a given level of ability dropping out after one year are nearly three times greater at the least selective colleges.

Tinto discusses the role of the peer group in preventing drop-out from college. Arguing on the basis of Durkheim's theory of suicide (i.e. suicide occurs when individuals are insufficiently integrated into the fabric of society), he claims that the motivated student will persist at college even if his academic record is poor and he relates little to other students. On the other hand, the unmotivated student who enjoys the social life will be more likely to be required to leave (i.e. failed) than to leave voluntarily. The student with both low academic achievement (i.e. poor grades and low motivation) and local social commitment (few or no friends) will drop out. Tinto argues that the 'peer group is the key for social integration' — the social relations the student enjoys may sustain him on the campus. In some cases, too, friends who are academically oriented can bring a student's academic and social perspectives closer together: one can think of an unmotivated student under social pressure from his flatmates to work for examinations so that the group can proceed into another year of study. Even one or two friends who are sympathetic may provide sufficient support to bring about reorientation.

Pantages and Creedon (1978) suggest that the peer group also plays a part in the student's decision to withdraw from college. Although most such decisions appear to be taken during the vacation (when relief at having temporarily finished with college is high and pressure to re-enrol is low), the process of contemplating withdrawal begins earlier and involves discussion with, first of all, friends of the same sex, secondly parents, and thirdly friends of the opposite sex. Discussion with staff is held normally *after* the decision to withdraw has been taken. Interestingly, too, staff do not strongly oppose students' wishes to withdraw in most cases: in fact they give rather weaker advice to continue in college than friends and parents.

This study also suggested that students talked over only a limited range of matters with staff, principally those relating to their courses, but were more likely to talk with friends and parents about academic difficulties, educational plans and purposes, vocational plans, religious beliefs and attitudes and values.

Several attempts have been made to differentiate between students on dimensions other than ability. Some students are relatively salient on the campus, and it has been suggested (e.g. Gamson, 1966) that, as at high school (Coleman, 1961), one can differentiate between members of the leading crowd and other sub-groupings. Scott (1965) showed that different groups subscribed to different sets of values: the majority of students, or the elite which regarded itself as most prestigious, held the dominant values, while minority groups (such as the Scripture Union) held 'variant' values. Deviants subscribed to practices such as drug taking which were generally disallowed and punished.

Reference has already been made in Chapter 2 to Clark and Trow's (1966) classification of student sub-cultures on the basis of two dimensions: student involvement with ideas and identification with college (see Figure 5.2).

Figure 5.2: Clark and Trow's (1966) Typology of Student Peer Groups

		involved with ideas	
		much	little
identify with college	much little	academic non-conformist	collegiate vocational

Both academic and non-conformist students are interested in ideas, but the former show this within the formal curriculum and identify with staff values. Non-conformists are more likely to be interested in ideas in the wider world of art, literature and politics, although Clark and Trow admit that they are a residual category including such diverse types as fashionable bohemians, hippies and apathetic alienated students.

Both collegiate and vocational students have little interest in intellectual matters *per se*. The collegiates hope to make the 'gentleman's C', to get a degree, but their main interest is in the social side of being a student; vocational students above all want their diplomas and will conform to satisfy the system, but have little interest in the ideas underlying their studies and no time to engage in extra-curricular activities. Attempts have been made by means of vignettes to operationalise the sub-cultures (e.g. Peterson, 1965a and 1965b) and these have shown substantial institutional differences in the percentage of students endorsing different options. Clark and Trow (1966) have suggested that the vocational orientation to college and learning is growing relatively stronger in the United States at the expense of the collegiate and academic orientations because of the greater relevance of academic qualifications with the expansion of higher occupations, educational mobility, bureaucratised academic contact, and reduced student residence and involvement in the life of the institution.

The Clark-Trow typology has stimulated a lot of discussion. It appears to suggest a neat way of categorising students, but not all students may recognise the vignettes as representing their character-istic attitude to the course and it may be that other categories are needed. Feldman and Newcomb (1969) suggest that Clark and Trow are describing types of student rather than types of sub-culture, but the latter reject this criticism and suggest that the student may participate in more than one 'sub-culture': they say that the norms and values of the sub-cultures are reflected in individuals in various blends. Bolton and Kammeyer (1972), however, argue that a sub-culture is normally thought of as an interacting group, where norms and values are transmitted and social control is exercised to ensure conformity to group norms. Sub-cultures, too, have different values from those of the parent group. Clark and Trow, they claim, have never demon-strated that the members of the different sub-cultures do interact — all that they have shown is that they are able to classify the students by the similarity of their sub-cultural orientation, and even here Bolton is able to show how slight differences in the wording of different vignettes can produce marked differences of response. Another criticism is that the dominant or parent culture from which the student sub-cultures are derived is undefined. We are left to guess whether it is the culture or values of the staff, the administration or society itself. It would be difficult to find consensus between these three groups. Nor, too, would it be correct to see the student sub-cultures as necessarily at variance with those of the staff: the academic, vocational and even collegiate values will, on occasions, be shared with the staff, and even non-conformist values may be supported by staff with Marxist or other radical orientations. Bolton and Kammeyer suggest that Clark and Trow are really highlighting role orientations of students rather than sub-cultures and they see three factors as distinguishing between such role orientations, viz. (1) the value the student places upon vocational preparation; (2) the extent of his intellectual-academic progress; and (3) the extent of his participation in campus social life. Finally they suggest that it may be more helpful to think of students in terms of different social types, such as the 'eager beaver' or the 'grind' who may perform in a characteristic way in any of the roles, academic or collegiate, that he adopts.

Students are likely to differ in the extent to which they mix with other students. But equally whom one mixes with may be important for academic performance and aspirations. Some evidence on these questions was provided by Wallace (1966) who conducted a questionnaire study of 327 first year students at a mid-west liberal arts college. On the second day on campus in September 1959 the students were asked questions about the value they attached to academic excellence, high grades and postgraduate study. As a measure of the students' interpersonal environment (IPE), they were presented with a list of the names of fellow students and asked to tick off those they recognised. Further questionnaires were administered to the whole student body in November 1959 and April 1960 and again information was collected on each student's IPE. Staff also completed a questionnaire.

Wallace found that students who became highly socially integrated into the peer group (as indicated by the number of the names they could recognise) tended to adopt its attitudes to grades and postgraduate study. Highly integrated first year students tended to become less concerned about the grades they were obtaining at present, but paradoxically more concerned about going on to postgraduate study. The pattern of change was, however, found to depend on the socio-economic ambition of both the student and the members of the peer group with whom he related.

It is likely that a student will get to know best (but not necessarily to like) those students with whom he interacts most: those who are taking the same subject and especially those with whom he works most frequently (e.g. in weekly tutorial or laboratory classes). Shared sporting or cultural interests are also likely to lead to interaction with other students, as is residence. Students who stay in hall, for example, will meet the same students continuously over a lengthy period and are likely to get to know several rather well.

Hatch (1968) has suggested a framework of interpretation for interactions in halls which may usefully be applied to thinking about the kinds of informal contact between students which is being discussed here. He suggested that halls could be characterised in terms of the range of activities which membership may involve (*scope*) and the degree of contact that exists within the hall (group, rank or hierarchial *cohesion*). Scope may be high or low: one can see the hall as simply a place for sleeping and eating, or it can involve one in a wide variety of roles. In the same way students' social life at college may differ in scope: the student living away from home may have higher scope than the student who commutes: not only will he be likely to be on campus for longer, but family and local friendship ties will not conflict with his ability to participate in extra-curricular university activities. Allbrow (1966), indeed, was able to show that hall students conversed more frequently about their academic work with fellow students, and attended more university societies and clubs than did students in lodgings. Although residence has not been found to correlate with academic performance, it is likely to lead to high scope since it makes it more likely that the student will associate with other students and staff and it will expose him to a wider variety of role models in both formal and informal situations from inside rather than outside the university.

Cohesion, too, may be high or low. 'Group' cohesion exists between friends who are frequently interacting; 'rank' cohesion refers to interaction between those of the same status; 'hierarchical' cohesion involves contacts between those occupying different status levels (e.g. warden and students). Cohesion will be greater in students who are physically and socially separated from other students and kept together over a long period of time. In a situation of sustained interaction such as was forced upon Becker's (1961) first year medical students, a common student culture is likely to develop among members of a class: a group identity is established and fostered by the fact that they have experiences in common. High scope need not be related to high group and rank cohesion: an individual may participate in a wide range of activities but with different groups of students, and may be inhibited about interacting with staff.

Institutions are likely to differ greatly in scope and cohesion and the atmosphere may change over time. Shipman (1969) reported how residence in a small college of education brought about great camaraderie between students, which led to a situation of high scope and high group, rank and hierarchical cohesion. As the student body grew in size, and a higher percentage of students lived off the campus, the situation changed: paradoxically, although there were more students available, the number of activities that could be sustained was smaller.

Becker's (1968) study highlights the role of the peer group in promoting personal and social development. Students at the University of Kansas defined 'maturity' in terms of the individual's ability both to maintain a requisite level of academic performance and to achieve in the peer group by dating and participating in a round of social activities. For the student, 'successful' adjustment to college encompassed both adequate academic achievement and fulfilment of an adequate social role. Becker reports how girls expressed serious dissatisfaction with the campus if the male students were too dedicated to work to date them: conversely, fraternity groups provided a service to assist students in academic difficulties to raise their performance so that they could meet the standard necessary for continued membership of the house.

The peer group, then, may be characterised in different ways. Its composition will change over time and this may affect its role in the institution. The nature of the peer group, and the individual's relationships within it, may have important influences on his academic success and on his sense of personal fulfilment.

Students' Perceptions of Learning from Peers

This chapter began with the claim that the peer group played an important part in the intellectual and moral development of the student. It is perhaps appropriate for it to end with evidence from a study by Wilson (1966) who asked final year students at Antioch College to state who or what had been influential in changing their thinking and outlook over their years at college, and what changes seemed significant to them. The data produced are admittedly tentative and crude, but they do appear to bear out the views of Perry

(1970) and Heath (1964).

The students identified over a dozen 'agents of change', and the large number of changes they specified (over 1,400 from 50 students) could be grouped into seven categories ranging from 'intellectual development' to 'world view and personal philosophy'. Of all the changes that had occurred 25 per cent were attributed to conventional academic sources (17 per cent to the 'impact of the course' and 8 per cent to staff), compared with 13 per cent to maturation and 10 per cent to peers. The conventional academic sources were also seen to be highly influential in respect of intellectual development (37 per cent) and the development of new tastes and interests (41 per cent). Peer group influence was responsible for around 10 per cent of the changes in world view, personal philosophy, personality, social development and attitude towards college, and contributed only 6 per cent to intellectual development. Perhaps the most striking finding, however, was that the students attached greatest importance to changes occurring in their world view and personal philosophy (40 per cent) and personality development (25 per cent) over their time in college, while intellectual development accounted for a mere 12 per cent of the changes reported and changes in career plans 5 per cent. In both of these salient aspects of change, fellow students were seen to exert a slightly greater influence than staff.

These data, then, do appear to confirm the importance of the peer group in student development. Wilson concludes that much of the change students undergo is not monitored by conventional academic assessment, and he suggests that it might be profitable to study the factors which determine with whom students associate and the nature of the effects. He proposes a taxonomic model which proceeds from general ascribed characteristics such as age and sex, via family context, to more specific achieved ones, including the characteristics of the pre-college peer group, personal traits and vocational plans.

Feldman and Newcomb (1969) sum up the role of the peer group in student learning as follows:

> they can help the individual achieve independence, support and facilitate the academic and intellectual goals of the college, offer general emotional support, and provide practice in getting along with people from different backgrounds. They can also provide the individual with support for doing what he has always done, or offer an alternative source of gratification, positive self-image and reward in non-academic ways.

It is clear that the student can learn a lot from other students. In the context of peer teaching, Goldschmid and Goldschmid quote Mac-Kenzie's (1970) remark that 'a student's colleagues often represent the least recognised, least used, and possibly the most important of all the resources available to him'. Students' attitudes to learning are likely to be more positive if group identity can be fostered; this may require staff to devote more time to teaching and to have more confidence in adopting a wider range of teaching methods. Reports such as *The Drift of Change* (Becher *et al.*, 1975) do suggest a perceptible shift towards student-centredness in teaching in many departments. The rewards certainly seem worth trying for. As one student in Parlett and King (1971) remarked:

I feel that a real feeling for a subject comes much more easily when there is a group identity: the enthusiasm and reassurance of the group rubs off on everyone. In this respect group identity is all important. In terms of simply memorising and learning subject matter group feeling has little or no effect.

The peer group effect is, then, largely an informal one, sustaining students in a variety of ways and some more than others. But writing essays, working out problems, reading and note-taking, and sitting examinations the student must ultimately tackle on his own. It is to the different ways in which students approach these tasks that we turn in the chapters which follow.

6 APPROACHES TO LEARNING

It is still common to talk of going up to 'read' history or physics at university. This refers, of course, to undertaking a course of study in a particular subject or field of knowledge. But reading — seeking out and grasping the meaning implicit in words or other symbolic representations — is one main access to facts and ideas and an important vehicle of learning. Like learning, too, reading is difficult to investigate because it is a private internal activity. Several recent studies have, however, sought to investigate how students approach different reading materials and the kinds of understanding they reach.

This topic was pursued in a series of interview studies carried out at the University of Gothenburg by Ference Marton and his colleagues. These focused on ways in which students read to learn typical prescribed materials in a situation where that learning was to be assessed. Consistent differences in the quality of understanding of students were related to the ways they read or 'processed' the text. 'Depth' processors sought out or created the meaning or 'thing signified' the author was trying to communicate. Their approach to reading was active and brought about qualitative change in their understanding of the subject matter. 'Surface' processors, on the other hand, paid attention to the more superficial features of the text. They read to remember facts, details and main arguments; their approach was passive in that they rarely examined the bases of conclusions, nor did they question the assumptions and logic of the argument. Reading to learn meant, for them, simply the addition of items of information to the memory store on a quantitative basis. Subsequent studies have suggested further distinctions within these two broad approaches.

British research has replicated and extended the early studies. Laurillard (1978) independently confirmed the depth-surface dimension and directed attention at the ways in which the context of learning affected the level of processing adopted by the student. Entwistle, Hanley and Ratcliffe (1979) have used questionnaires to assess students' approach, but only preliminary results have so far been reported.

Background to the Gothenburg Studies

The Gothenburg studies have followed a common pattern in that all students are asked to read and answer questions about a set text. Some experimental manipulation has, however, been attempted with the aim of inducing students to adopt a particular approach to the reading task. The materials used have included edited chapters of books, newspaper articles and home produced papers of similar complexity. Average length is 3,000 words. Samples are small, consisting of around 30 first year students, mostly girls, who are paid volunteers. No background information, personality or intellectual correlates are reported. The procedure adopted is for the student to study the set text, without time limit, in a one-to-one tape-recorded situation with the experimenter. She then answers oral and/or written questions about her understanding of the text, and gives an introspective account of how she has read it. Students are told the 'correct' answer if they are unable to give a satisfactory explanation to any of the questions which test understanding. Long-term recall is also tested between five and seven weeks later.

Students' answers are classified at one of four or five levels by the experimenter and a colleague independently. Allocation to depth and surface level of processing is also done independently, and dichotomously in all studies except one (Marton and Säljö, 1976a).

Several studies have introduced specific 'experimental' features. Marton and Säljö (1976b), for example, inserted depth and surface questions at the end of two successive chapters of Coombs in the expectation that students, who had previously been allocated at random to one or other of these conditions, would read a third chapter at that level. All students (N=40) were in fact set a common 'summarising' task, followed by specific questions on content. Fransson (1977) ingeniously sought to control for intrinsic and extrinsic motivation, as well as level of anxiety. But his assumption that material describing the Institute's examination system would be of higher relevance (intrinsic motivation) to its education students than to sociology students was mistaken: many of the sociology students found the material more interesting. He also obtained self-ratings on test anxiety, and put the students (N=81) into groups of three to five under tense and relaxed conditions. Half the groups were led to believe that one student would be asked to lead a taped discussion on the text (strong extrinsic motivation); the other half (weak extrinsic motivation) that there would be a general discussion of the paper after each participant had written down what he could remember of it. All students in fact simply summarised the paper and completed a 15-item short answer test, before being interviewed on how they had reacted to the experiment. Because the experimental conditions were not fulfilled, considerable weight was given to the students' interpretation of the situation in the analysis.

Svensson (1977) related cognitive approach to normal study habits and success in university examinations. Data were collected on two related texts on curriculum reform in the Swedish universities at three sessions, each five weeks apart. The first text had been used previously by Marton and Säljö (1976a); the second was three times longer. In this experiment, which was part of a larger investigation of study methods, recall and introspective explanations were followed by specific questions on the text and probes about characteristic ways of tackling normal class work. The second and third sessions began with a re-test of the text studied in the previous session. Data were also collected on the students' examination performance.

Both Fransson's and Marton and Säljö's (1976b) studies have flawed experimental design. In the latter, the initial condition of *random* allocation to a particular treatment seems inappropriate: the important question is whether known depth-processors can be induced to adopt surface styles and vice versa. Some students may already have been processing at the level towards which they were supposedly being induced.

Laurillard both replicated Marton's 'set task' technique, on a passage by Bertrand Russell, and then extended the scope of the inquiry by asking students of technology to describe their approach to reading and problem solving with materials they were actually using in their course work. She then analysed the students' recorded accounts of how they tackled this work using Marton's criteria for depth and surface processing.

Entwistle *et al.* (1979) conducted pilot experiments in which university students and sixth formers were set to read passages by Cyril Burt, Fred Hoyle and Maya Pines under 'relaxed examination conditions' (40 minutes for a 4,000 word article). Then they took a short test of creativity before answering questions about the content of the article and their method of reading it. Students were asked to describe the article as if to a friend who had not read it, to rate it for interest and novelty of ideas, to answer specific questions about the content, and finally to describe their study approach and say whether, in normal studying, it was similar or different to the one they had adopted. Approach and general level of understanding were assessed on a three point scale. The criteria for approach were similar to those described by Marton and Laurillard: understanding was signified by the student (a) reinterpreting and reorganising what he had read, rather than simply recalling points in the order read, (b) mentioning 'sufficient' of the main points and (c) showing that he had grasped the gist of the article.

Levels of Understanding

The Gothenburg studies demonstrate very clear differences in qualitative understanding of ideas and principles. As Marton and Säljö (1976a) have noted: 'a highly significant aspect of learning is the variation in what is learned, i.e. the diversity of ways in which the same phenomenon, concept or principle is apprehended by different students'.

The best way to illustrate the point is by considering the task set in one of the studies (Marton and Säljö, 1976a) and the different levels of answer elicited from the students.

In one of our experiments we asked 40 female first-termers to read three incomplete chapters from Coombs: *The World Educational Crisis: A Systems Analysis* (1971, Swedish edition). The basic aim of the third of these chapters is to give the reader a thorough understanding of the effects of education on individuals and society — the output of educational systems. The point which the author wants to make in this connection can be seen from the following quotation:

It is impossible to measure with any presently known gauge the full output and eventual impact of an educational system. Some sense of what is involved can be grasped if we imagine a school whose whole output consists of a single student. On the day he graduates, what kind of an output does he embody? The answer is that he embodies a multiplicity of outputs — represented, for instance, in the facts and concepts he has learned, the style of thinking he has acquired, and also such changes as may have occurred in his outlook, values, ambitions, and personal conduct. If one then asks how all this will affect the future life of this student, his family and society, the difficulty is several times compounded. Such cause and effect relationships are often as indistinct as a line drawn through water. But if these matters are hard to get at in the case of a single student, they are infinitely more elusive when the matter to be judged is the output represented by multiple streams of individuals, flowing through different educational channels for different lengths of time. (Coombs, 1971)

In subsequent pages Coombs argues against the simplified notion of output of educational systems as being equal to the number of people who pass their exams. He stresses the need for a large number of criteria in assessing the real influence of education on society.

In order to check whether the students had understood what the author wanted to say with regard to the output of educational systems the following question was posed:

'What is meant by the output of an education system?' The words used in the answers to this question varied very much, but eventually we saw that students had adopted four basically rather different ways of comprehending what is meant by the output of an educational system. We shall call these four different types of answer levels of outcome which are thus concrete examples of qualitative differences in learning. The following classification presents what was understood at each of these levels together with two typical answers to illustrate the explanations given by the students.

Level A: The Effects of Education on Society and on Individuals Produced by Knowledge and Attitudes Acquired through Schooling

'Mm, that's terribly difficult to answer. There was this example about how if you just had one pupil and wanted to work out the output, it would depend on so many things. . .or factors, or whatever facts or concepts it was about. . .whether he has completed his education, what his own viewpoint is. . .and everything that is going to influence his life later on and that sort of thing. . .and his productivity, suitability. . .'

'Mm, it's the knowledge that. . .and values. . .yes, the knowledge and values that students have acquired. That is, whatever it is that influences them and makes them read this or that and do this or that.'

Level B: Those Who Leave the Educational System With or Without a Qualification

'Well, those who have been to school and gone right through the course, and even those who've failed, they're a sort of output, too.'

'Well, it's those who pass their final exams, that is, well not necessarily pass, but those who take part in the course even if they drop out at some point, you know. . .those who have taken part and then dropped out.'

Level C: Those Who Leave the Educational System with a Completed Education.

'It's the pupils who have gone right through the system from start to finish.'

'It's the trained work-force that the educational system produces. It's well, for example. . .well, simply the trained work-force.'

Level D: What Comes Out of the Educational System.

'Something to do with. . .well. . .you know, the result of.'

'The product. . .I think.'

The levels of outcome, i.e. different ways of comprehending what the author meant by 'output of education', can be said to constitute the outcome space for this particular question in relation to the present text. Those answers which were categorised (by two independent judges) as belonging to level A are clearly the best since they contain the intentional content of the author's argument with evidence which shows that the subjects have grasped the more elaborate way of looking at 'output' that the author wishes to convey to the reader. The B level answers contain a part of the intentional content since they include in 'output' not only those who pass, but also those who drop out somewhere during their education, and the author considers this to be a very important aspect of the output of educational systems. On level C we find answers which merely include those who pass through the complete educational system. This is the most common conception of output and is, in fact, precisely the conception which the author wants to argue against, since the real and important aspects of output are of a quite different nature from the mere number of people who pass. In fact, those students who gave a C level answer have given an explanation of output which is the exact opposite of the one the author intends to give the reader. The D level answers, finally, are virtually empty of content and in most cases they merely contain a translation of the term 'output'. The fact that this chapter was an attempt to give the reader a more sophisticated understanding of the concept of 'output' thus seems to have completely escaped these students.

In all of the investigations it has been possible to identify similar qualitative differences in outcome. In some (e.g. Svensson, 1977; Fransson, 1977), differentiation has depended on the extent to which students could link facts and arguments to the author's conclusions. Fransson (1977), for example, found that students' replies could be placed in the following four categories:

(a) conclusion-oriented, content. The student summarises his main conclusions from reading the text. He explains his thoughts and reflections while reading the text, and summarises the parts of information that he has found most interesting.

(b) conclusion-oriented, mentioning. The student reports that he has found certain parts of the information sheet interesting, but he does not summarise the contents of these parts.

(c) description, content. The student has tried to give a neutral and complete summary of the content of the text.

(d) description, mentioning. The student has intended to write a complete list of content of the text.

Entwistle (personal communication) found that he was able to distinguish between his students' accounts of their reading on the same basis: one of his students simply copied out the first three paragraphs of the set article, while others made a list of main ideas without any attempt to connect them up; others, again, wrote accounts which reinterpreted the article in their own terms.

Most studies report data on student performance and, although different texts are involved and the learning situation was manipulated in some cases, it is of interest to see what proportion of students give satisfactory (levels A and B) and unsatisfactory (levels C and D) accounts in each experiment (see Table 6.1).

One interesting finding not reported in the table is that students' level of understanding appears to remain remarkably stable on the recall test some weeks later. Those who have initially grasped the main point of an article retain that understanding, whereas those who have been 'told' the correct version can recall only their original impression. Some general loss of information does, of course, occur: recalls are generally 'more inexact and fragmentary', and there is a tendency to move from a depth to a surface level of processing. A more perplexing finding is that in two of the studies (Marton and Säljö, 1976b; Svensson, 1977) a few students actually improve their performance.

Table 6.1: Level of Outcome of Students on Selected Learning Tasks in the Immediate Recall Situation

| | Gothenburg Studies | | | | | |
| | Marton and Saljo (1976a) | | Marton and Saljo (1976b) | Fransson (1977) | Svensson (1977) | |
Level of outcome	a1 N(%)	a2 N(%)	b1 N(%)	c1 N(%)	d1[a] N(%)	d2 N(%)
Satisfactory (A,B)	12(34)	16(53)	18(64)	27(33)	*	19(63)
Unsatisfactory (C,D)	23(66)	14(47)	10(36)	54(67)		11(37)
All	35(100)	30(100)	28(100)	81(100)		30(100)
	NI = 4		NI = 9			

Learning tasks: a1. 'What is meant by the outcome of an education system?' (Coombs)
a2. Recall and summary question on article on university reform. (home-made)
b1. 'Why does the selective system as a rule have a higher pass rate?' (Coombs)
c1. Free recall summary on examinations at the Institute of Education, University of Gothenburg. (home-made)
d2. Free recall on article on university reform. (home-made)

Note: a. Svensson's first sample is the same as Marton and Saljo's a2.

These results, then, indicate that many first year students have difficulty in grasping the main points expressed in a passage: they reach different levels of understanding of the principal ideas. The question next to be considered is whether such differences in understanding are related to the ways in which students read.

The Process of Learning and its Relationship to Understanding

The distinction between depth and surface processors (Marton and Säljö, 1976a) and atomists and holists (Svensson, 1977) is based on the analysis of students' introspective accounts of how they read the passages set in the experiments. Students had to describe what they thought about as they were reading, which aspects they concentrated on, and how far they tried to memorise specific facts and details.

The two approaches appear to reflect different conceptions of 'what it takes to learn'. Marton (1975) explains the difference as follows:

> For some, learning is the grasping of what the discourse is about, i.e. learning is learning through the discourse, and for others, learning is learning the discourse (i.e. memorising it). The former appear to experience an active role (i.e. learning is something they do); the latter do not appear to do this (learning is something that happens to them). (Marton, 1975)

Depth learners tackled the assignments in an active, questioning way. They tried to make sense of what they were reading, scutinising it intently, almost savaging it to extract its central meaning. Here are some typical comments:

> '. . .I tried to look for. . .you know, the principal ideas. . .'
> 'I tried to think what it (the article) was all about. . .I thought how he had built up the whole thing.'
> 'I went back to find the connections. . .'
> 'I kept the previous page in mind while reading the next. . .'

Depth learners, then, linked facts and arguments to conclusions. They 'thought about', 'tried to get at', the author's meaning through the words in which he had clothed his ideas. They were interested in the communication as a whole, and worried at it until they got 'the point of it'. Svensson (1977) found that this general approach was typical of how these students tackled their everyday academic work. In their studies they were concerned to identify 'the central point', 'what it boils down to', 'the total picture', and again they did so in an active way. They tried to 'connect the new and the old', 'build up the structure', 'draw conclusions', 'reflect on the logic of the argument', 'question the truth of the statement', etc. In tackling examinations, one student described how he reordered his data to be able to cope with the question:

> One builds up a sort of construction, a frame you could say, figuratively speaking. A book — one has a frame for it and to that certain associations; and then come the questions that do not — absolutely do not fit in. The whole thing collapses, and then one has to begin again and build up a new structure that will stand up to those questions, and there you have it — it has changed. (Svensson, 1977)

Depth learners also interrelate subject matter and make links between their academic studies and the 'real' world beyond the university. 'Book learning', knowledge, concepts, and rules of procedure developed through academic studies shape their personal frame of reference and increase their level of sophistication.

Surface learners' accounts of how they read are strikingly different. Some appeared to be very anxious and found it hard to concentrate on the content:

> '. . .I didn't remember what I read, because I was just thinking of hurrying on. . .'
> '. . .I was thinking about the fact that I was going to have to repeat all this. . .I didn't think out what I was reading. . .'
> 'The whole time I was thinking "now I must remember this" and "now I must remember this". . .'

But these descriptions also point to one of the characteristic features of the surface learner: his reproductive conception of learning which results in a rote learning strategy. Their recalls stay close to the sequence of ideas and even wording of the original passage. Surface learners pay attention only to the superficial features of the text: they read passively, unreflecting, as if unaware that understanding involves effort. Consider the following comments:

'. . .It was words. . .you didn't have to think about what they meant, it was just a matter of reading straight through.'
'. . .I just read straight through without looking back at anything. . .'
'. . .It wasn't so much that I drew conclusions. . .and reacted to them. . .but that, well, that I read it sort of because I was supposed to read it. . .and not so as to react to it.'

Such observations imply an unreflective attitude to study. Surface learners do not link up ideas within their studies, or relate their learning to external reality. Marton's criteria for distinguishing between depth and surface processors follow (from Laurillard, 1978).
Depth processors focus on:
(1) the intention of the article (author)
(2) actively trying to integrate what they read with previous parts of the argument (text)
(3) trying to use their own ability to make a logical construction
(4) thinking about the functional role of the different parts of an argument.
Surface processors focus on:
(1) the time factor instead of the task
(2) the demand to perform instead of the actual task
(3) learning which is equated with memorising
(4) the subject, confronting the text passively and treating it as an isolated phenomenon (read without thinking)
(5) the subject, keeping their reading to the surface of the text without any relation to the meaning.

An important distinction within these general approaches is made by Fransson (1977) and confirmed by Entwistle *et al.* (1979). Fransson talks of differences in level of attention (high and low), while Entwistle refers to 'active' and 'passive' approaches. Fransson comments: 'within each level of processing some subjects were working very intensively, while others seemed to be satisfied by forming a general impression'. The distinction seems to be of particular importance for two sub-groups: deep students working at low levels of attention, and surface students working at high levels. The former 'tried to form a general impression of the information material in order to be able to return to the text when their need for this special information became more pressing': the latter 'tried to press the text into their minds'.

Table 6.2: Level of Processing by Level of Outcome on Learning Tasks in the Immediate Recall Situation

I Level of processing reported in Gothenburg studies

Level of outcome	Marton and Säljö (1976a)			Svensson (1977)			
				(1)[b]		(2)	
	Surface	Not clear	Deep[a]	Atomists	Holists	Atomists	Holists
Satisfactory (A,B)	1	6	9	1	14	3	16
Unsatisfactory (C,D)	13	1	0	13	1	10	1
All	14	7	9	14	15	13	17

II Fransson (1977)

	Surface		Depth	
	High attention	Low attention	High attention	Low attention
Conclusion - content	3	-	6	9
Conclusion - mentioning	3	-	3	3
Description - content	20	4	9	9
Description - mentioning	4	1	-	7
Total	30	5	18	28

Notes: a. Includes one subject showing indications of both.
b. Svensson's first sample is the same as Marton and Säljö's reported above.

The data summarising the relationship between level of processing and level of outcome are presented in Table 6.2. Svensson's results are included because of the obvious conceptual similarities between atomists and holists, and surface and depth processors: Svensson justifies his terminology because he believes it emphasises the 'unity of knowledge and cognitive skill', and eliminates the distinction, implicit in the earlier studies, between 'achievement' and 'process'.

The table shows that the proportion of students identified as depth and surface processors varies markedly between studies. The intermediate category, too, disappears although earlier Marton (1975) had emphasised that 'the two levels...are not to be considered as two distinct and separate categories. Rather they imply a dimension along which individuals vary'. Fransson reported that his judges found it hard to categorise 26 per cent of his sample, and it is possible that describing the data dichotomously is inappropriate.

Marton and Säljö (1976a) and Svensson (1977) show a strong association between depth processing and high understanding. Both Laurillard and Entwistle also found some evidence that depth learners were better at writing summaries and other tasks involving understanding. On the Hoyle article Entwistle reported correlations of +0.45 between level of understanding and a depth approach, and –0.29 with a surface approach, but the relationship was in general weaker than Marton claimed. In Fransson's study the relationship is also much weaker (and not significant statistically). Other results from this study show that level of attention is not related clearly to understanding on a free recall summary, but deep level learners reading at a high level of attention are significantly better than other groups on a factual knowledge test. What is specially striking in Table 6.2, however, is the distribution of Fransson's students working at different levels of attention over the outcome categories. The majority of the surface learners are working at high levels of attention, and this leads them to give complete neutral descriptive summaries of what they have read. However, just under half of the 'deep' students also provide descriptive accounts, although their approach is clearly compatible with 'conclusion oriented accounts'. The implication here is that, with complex reading materials, depth processors will provide the kind of response they believe to be appropriate to the demands of the test situation, while surface processors are limited to giving descriptive accounts of what they have read.

Level of Processing: Fixed or Variable?

An obvious question stemming from the research is the extent to which individuals have access to both of these levels of processing and the factors which induce depth processing. To this may be linked a general question about the flexibility of study strategies. Do students vary their approach consciously in the light of the perceived demands of the learning task?

One piece of relevant evidence concerns whether the nature of the assessment affects the kind of revision students undertake. If, for example, students know they are to be examined by multiple choice questions, does this cause them to adopt a strategy which is different from the one they would follow for an essay-type examination? One answer appears to be that it does not: a study by Hakstian (1971) showed that students tend to adopt the same approach to revision irrespective of the nature of the anticipated examination.

This evidence fits in with what Svensson found. He suggested that students had a consistent 'cognitive approach': 'holists' on one text are also likely to adopt a 'holistic' strategy on the next and in normal study. Twenty-five of his students reached a similar level of understanding on both texts on immediate recall, and 17 of these were consistent on delayed recall as well.

Other studies, however, indicate that particular learning strategies can be manipulated. Marton and Säljö (1976b), who tried to induce surface and depth processing by means of questions placed at the end of each passage, found that surface processing was more readily induced. Some surface learners had expected only surface level questions, while others reported modifying their regular learning strategies. Some depth processors 'technified' learning in the sense that they read primarily to fulfil the 'recall and summarise' demands of the questions. These students are reminiscent of Fransson's deep 'low attention' students; they simply devised a technique which at a superficial level met the requirements. Most of the other students did adopt a more thorough depth treatment, although the questions set were not as effective as had been hoped. One student, who demonstrated the desired effects, commented: 'I got some help as to *how* to read the piece. The questions you asked me put me on to a good way of reading the piece somehow.' It may be that these differences within the groups can be explained in terms of experimental design.

Fransson's results are not clear cut but he also showed some evidence of adaptation, and concluded that a subject with high trait anxiety

> motivated by test demands to read a text for which he has very limited interest is very probable to adopt a surface learning strategy, while deep level learning seems to be the normal strategy chosen by a student motivated only by the relevance of the content of the text to his personal needs and interests.

Deep level processing was likely to occur under relaxed learning conditions where the subject was intrinsically interested in the subject matter. If Fransson is correct, it is perhaps not surprising that such a high proportion of the students adopted surface strategies in the Gothenburg studies!

Cognitive Approach and Normal Studying

Svensson collected information about the number of hours students worked, how they normally tackled assignments and revised for examinations, as well as their examination performance, and related these data to cognitive approach. He found high agreement between the approach used in the experiments and that reported for normal studies: 13 of the students were consistent 'atomists' and 10 consistent 'holists'.

Figure 6.1: Differentiation between Students who Passed and Failed an Examination in Education in Relation to Information about their Approaches to Studying

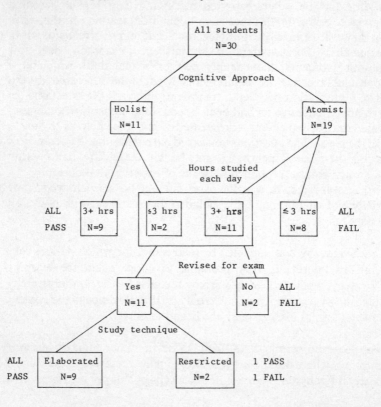

Svensson distinguishes between students who display an 'elaborated' as opposed to a 'restricted' study technique. An elaborated technique involves making summaries, underlining important parts of books, and making extensive use of lecture notes. Combining information on cognitive approach, hours studied each day, revision for examination and study technique, he was able to predict examination performance correctly for 29 of the 30 students (see Figure 6.1).

The poor performance of atomists is striking. Svensson attributes their lack of success to their emphasis on memorising material and over-learning as opposed to understanding. The drudgery involved in their approach may pay off over long hours of application, but if motivation falls, and fewer hours are worked, their performance will suffer.

Laurillards's evidence suggested that many students use both approaches according to their interpretation of the demands of the learning situation. Only 12 of her 32 students used a consistently deep approach, while 19 used both styles on different occasions. The following extract illustrates how a student — Chris — can adopt different styles for different learning tasks and maintain them consistently in accordance with his perception of what he needs to do to fulfil the demands of the task.

Deep Level Processing
'This has to be handed in — it's an operation research exercise, a programme to find a minimum point on a curve. First I had to decide on the criteria of how to approach it, then drew a flow diagram, and checked through each stage. You have to think about it and understand it first. I used my knowledge of O.R. design of starting with one point, testing it and then judging the next move. I try to work through logically. Putting in diagrams helps you think clearly and follow through step by step. I chose this problem because it was more applied, more realistic. You can learn how to go about O.R. You get an idea of the different types of problem that exist from reading.' *Chris: Problem A*

Surface Level Processing
'This problem is not to be handed in, but it will be discussed in the lecture because the rest of the course depends on this kind of thing. I knew how I'd do it from looking at it, it practically tells you what equation to use. You just have to bash the numbers out. I knew how to do it before I started so I didn't get anything out of it. There's not

really any thinking. You just need to know what you need to solve the problem. I read through the relevant notes, but not much, because you don't need to look at the system. It's really just a case of knowing what's in the notes, and choosing which block of notes to use. You don't have to interpret it in terms of the system. It's only when things go wrong, you have to think about it then. In this sort of situation you've just to get through to the answer.' *Chris: Problem B*

Laurillard makes an important point when she observes that Chris's surface approach to Problem B does not necessarily imply, as Marton appears to suggest, a passive or unconscious role for the learner. Rather it is the case that the approach adopted is perceived by the student to be adequate to the needs of the situation.

Laurillard, then, argues that, while the depth-surface dichotomy exists, most students may use both approaches, and the one that is adopted will reflect the student's interpretation of the kind of investment of mental energy that is necessary for successful accomplishment of the learning task in question.

Ramsden (1979) has also produced evidence that the approach used in essay writing and problem solving depends greatly on the student's background knowledge and level of interest in the task, the former being of particular importance in science and the latter in arts and social science. But the student's personal commitment seems also to be important, as this quotation from an independent studies student at Lancaster illustrates:

In reading a particular bit of the book that I thought was relevant I was relating it to the overall arguments within that book. . .and also relating it to the overall directions of the independent studies project I was doing. But that particular approach was a product of my desire to sort of do a bit of creative, original work. Had I been writing a straight essay, which I did in my first unit. . . I probably would have just, sort of, taken out the main points and strung them together. . .there's a definite difference between reading a book with the objective of simply summarising the argument and reading a book with the objective of actually using those arguments for your own ends.

Conclusion

The studies reported in this chapter have been concerned with how students read or mentally 'process' texts whose level of difficulty is similar to that encountered in normal academic work, what level of understanding they reach, and the relationship between these two factors. The significance and implications of the findings obviously depend on the validity of the methods by which the data were collected.

One central problem in the study of learning is how to externalise the process by which learning occurs. Bruner *et al.* (1956) suggest that introspective recall is not a satisfactory technique: they found that most of their subjects could not recall accurately how they attempted tasks of concept acquisition 'although the sequence of behaviour showed systematic features of a highly regular and skilled order'. The Gothenburg studies simply tell us about how students think they read the texts in question: they do not show us how they in fact did read them. At the same time their accounts do have *some* validity, and the performance evidence is consistent with the approaches they claim to have adopted. Laurillard, however, criticises Marton's research design as atheoretical: some relationship appears to exist between process and outcome, but the nature and cause of that relationship are not clarified by the studies, nor do they themselves reflect a theoretical model of student learning.

Related criticisms can be levelled at the way the data were collected and analysed. Anyone who has worked with first-term girls, at least in Scotland, would expect them, paid or not, to be apprehensive when put in a one-to-one 'read and answer' situation with a lecturer. The disturbingly high proportion of surface processors could partly be explained by the induction of unintended stress. The depth-surface distinction, too, was identified much more clearly from interviews than from questionnaires, which may reflect the opportunity for probing questioning, but Entwistle criticised Marton's use of a disjunctive system of classification whereby *any* indication of 'depth' or 'surface' thinking was taken as a justification for allocating a student to a particular category. He also cautioned Fransson for accepting expressed interest or anxiety at its face value. Entwistle highlighted the crucial importance of the text selected: it 'should contain a closely reasoned argument supported by detailed factual evidence, and needs to be challenging for the more knowledgeable, while being accessible to students new to the topic' (Entwistle *et al.*, 1979). It is, therefore, apparently only with intellectually demanding reading material that distinct approaches can be identified.

Only the studies by Svensson and Laurillard attempted to relate the student's approach in the experimental situation to normal studying, but the latter's invitation to students to describe assignments they were working on was too open-ended to allow comparisons to be made across tasks of different importance or interest, or to relate approach to level of understanding.

Given these weaknesses, what do the findings themselves amount to? In some ways the depth-surface distinction is reminiscent of that made by Bloom *et al.* (1956) between lower and higher order educational objectives: on this view surface learners are working at the level of recall, the lowest level in the taxonomy, while depth learners are capable of working at the higher levels as well. The early studies confirm the distinction between depth and surface processors (holists and atomists), and show a strong association with 'high' and 'low' levels of understanding. Both Fransson and Entwistle, however, introduce distinctions within these approaches, and specify 'levels of outcome' as 'conclusion-oriented' or 'descriptive'. Their results suggest that the relationship between process and outcome is weaker: some students appear to have access to both levels of processing and depth students adopt a 'technified' approach to fulfil the demands of the question as they perceive it. This leads the majority to provide 'descriptive' accounts because they think this is the kind of answer expected of them. There are echoes here of the hidden curriculum.

The several findings on depth and surface processing can be brought together as follows. The initial position described by Marton (1975), Marton and Säljö (1976a) and Svensson (1977) was that students could be classified as either surface (atomist) or depth (holist) processors. Fransson's (1977) results suggested that all students could surface-process, but only some could depth-process; surface processing could be induced by the learning context and factors such as stress. Laurillard and Ramsden went further by suggesting that most students could use a surface or a depth approach, depending on their perception of the context. But this claim may reflect the particular students they studied. Ramsden's sample was second year, and it may be that by then all students *have* developed a depth approach. Developing a depth approach may be a condition of academic survival! Entwistle (1979) accepted that students may have access to both approaches, but argued that they may also have a preferred or characteristic approach to study in general: some students are more likely to search for meaning in their reading than others. Entwistle, like Marton, lays considerable stress on the way the student interprets the instructions and learning task, and maintains that this creates an intention to learn in a certain way. Intention is reflected in the level of processing.

But is not the student's *conception* of what learning involves, rather than his intention, one of the most important factors which will affect the approach he adopts? First year students are likely to have relatively simple conceptions of what it takes to learn, and that may be why so many engage in such inefficient practices as making copperplate versions of their lecture notes. Their conception of learning is likely to be founded on their school experiences and perhaps their 'stage' of intellectual development.

On this view, then, all students do have the potential to adopt depth as well as surface approaches. The approach they actually do adopt will depend upon several factors. First is likely to be the difficulty of the subject matter: some texts can be skimmed over while others can only be understood by systematically setting out the arguments, evidence and conclusions. Second is the interest and importance of the text: a 'set' book will receive a closer look than supplementary reading, but especially if its subject matter appeals to the student. Third may be the student's natural preference for reading in a particular way: the studies so far reported have not really clarified whether there are in fact basic differences in approach or whether the approaches actually used reflect the fourth factor, viz. the student's conception of what it takes to learn complex subject matter. One of the functions of study skills courses is to change these conceptions by means of consciousness-raising techniques such as Thomas and Harri-Augstein describe in *The Art and Science of Getting a Degree*. But the substitution of qualitatively different conceptions of what it means to learn may be a process which the student is not conscious of, even in retrospect.

To some extent, as Entwistle and Hanley (1977) have pointed out, these studies are simply 'rediscovering the wheel'. Isaac Watts, writing in 1810, describes differences between learners which are remarkably similar to 'depth' and 'surface' processing.

It is meditation and study that transfers and conveys the notions and sentiments of others to ourselves, so as to make them properly our own. It is our own judgement upon them, as well as our memory of them, that makes them become our own property... By study and meditation we improve the hints that we have acquired by observation, conversation, and reading: we take more time in thinking, and by the labour of the mind we penetrate deeper into the themes of knowledge. . .

There are many who read with constancy and diligence, and yet make no advances in true knowledge by it. They are delighted with the notions which they read or hear, as they would be with stories that are told, but they do not weigh them in their minds as in a just balance, in order to determine their truth or falsehood; they make no observations upon them. Perhaps their eye slides over the pages, or the words slide over their ears, and vanish like a rhapsody of evening tales, or the shadow of a cloud flying over a green field in a summer's day. (Watts, 1810)

But the distinction between depth and surface processing is only one feature of these studies; of equal importance is the way they highlight how students fail to learn. One cause is misunderstanding of basic ideas. Dahlgren and Marton (1976) stress that teaching should start, as the progressives have always argued, 'where the learner is'. They suggest that a course in economics, for example, should explore the apparently trivial questions such as 'why does a bun cost what it does?' because considerable meaning is involved in supplying the answer, it illustrates fundamental economic concepts, and it provides a link with the everyday world which is familiar to first year students. An examination of the conceptual demands of a subject necessarily focuses on its language and this is a means to clarifying student misconceptions. A British study with similar objectives in the field of biology (Burchill, 1978) may help to illuminate the difficulties encountered by students at the transition from school to university.

There is a slightly incestuous air about the Gothenburg research: a small group of colleagues, sharing common assumptions, 'independently' categorise students and even rework each other's data. The results raise more questions than they answer. Further research needs to be directed at one issue in particular: the nature of the interventions in student learning that would assist first year students to embrace the active, questioning role of the depth processor which is essential for the achievement of what most people would recognise as understanding.

7 LEARNING AND UNDERSTANDING COMPLEX IDEAS

How do people go about learning complex new fields of knowledge and the structure of ideas within them? Or, to be more specific, how do students master unfamiliar ideas in an article or a textbook? Alice's advice was straightforward: 'Begin at the beginning, and go on to the end, and then stop.' Observations of students in the library suggest that many do just that: they read page after page systematically, often taking copious notes, and when they reach the end they thankfully snap the book shut and over coffee talk about something else. The ideas remain within the text, or their notes, but are not worked over in their minds. Equally, however, one can observe students whose strategy is quite different: they read around whatever their eye happens to light upon, searching back and forwards in the text for points of interest, moving from topic to topic in an apparent attempt to get the gist of the subject without the chore of reading every word.

The work of Gordon Pask and his associates at Richmond has been particularly ingenious and stimulating in suggesting how these processes might be studied. They have devised original complex learning tasks and artificial learning environments. Students start from a common base and the conditions under which they learn can be manipulated to explore individual differences and the effects of context on the quality of learning. Learning is conceived of as a conversation which may be internal, between teacher and taught, or between the student and a computerised map of a field of knowledge. Two basic strategies have been identified. 'Serialists' approach a learning task on a step by step basis; 'holists' attempt to see the task globally. These strategies are most apparent in free or uncontrolled learning situations, such as reading a textbook or learning a taxonomy from cards. If teaching is matched to the learner's strategy, it produces strikingly successful learning. The strategies are held to be manifestations of more general 'operational' or 'comprehension' learning styles. Success in the variety of tasks of everyday learning demands 'versatility', i.e. the ability to select the appropriate combination of styles for the task in hand. Pask maintains that 'understanding' is achieved in controlled learning situations only by insisting on the most stringent performance criteria.

The Representation of Ideas

The ideas of a subject constitute the material for learning. Ideas may be represented in a variety of ways. Bruner (1966) suggests three modes of representation: enactive (doing), ikonic (visual) and symbolic (words or numbers). Symbolic representation in language is the most common way of communicating ideas: we talk of 'equality of opportunity', 'the normal curve', 'dyslexia', 'polysomy', 'progress', 'drink' — even the last of these abstract concepts summarises a mass of specific subordinate knowledge and expresses relationships within that knowledge which are not self-evident and which the student may be expected to become familiar with. In the sciences task analysis (Gagné, 1965), which was particularly influential in the development of programmed learning, has led to ikonic representation of ideas in a 'knowledge hierarchy' or family tree of related concepts identified on the basis of logical and psychological analysis.

Figure 7.1: Entailment Structure for 'drink'

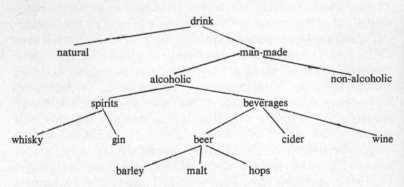

In Figure 7.1 a conceptual taxonomy or entailment structure for 'drink' has been defined. To 'entail' implies a legal and logical relationship: the higher, more abstract concepts inevitably and inescapably subsume and follow on from the lower, more concrete ones. One advantage of representing a complex idea in this way is that prerequisite or subordinate knowledge and skills can be more readily identified and incorporated into the teaching process; but another is that it becomes possible to study how students come to understand a particular concept, and to identify where further simplification or alternative representation of an idea is required.

It is, of course, not always possible to present ideas in a taxonomic model. In a psychiatric or social context 'drink' would require different conceptualisation. Similarly in the arts and social sciences it is likely that concepts are interdependent rather than hierarchically related. In history, the vocabulary of the subject includes 'power', 'revolution', 'era', 'conquest', 'constitution', and these ideas are difficult to explain except in terms of each other. Nevertheless it is possible to set out different ideas and to see how they connect up. Thomas and Harri-Augstein (1978) and Pask (1976b) have encouraged students to construct personal 'meaning nets' These networks may play a role similar to mnemonics in rote learning. Figure 7.2 shows 35 salient features of the reign of Henry VIII which Pask asked students participating in a 'learning to learn' experiment to connect up on the basis of perceived links.

The representation of ideas may both help the teacher to structure his communication and clarify what the student has to learn, but an important consolidating factor in learning is the stringency of the requirement to reach 'understanding'. The student listening to a lecture or undertaking background reading by the fireside is in a 'free learning' situation where any test of understanding is self-imposed. In experimental learning situations the criterion of understanding is often performance on a multiple-choice test. Such tests more often measure recognition or recall than productive thinking. Pask argues for more stringent criteria. One of these is effective verbal teachback where the student has to reteach an idea to his tutor until he has got it 'right'; another is performance of the skill which has been learned.

The point here is that these criteria force the learner to behave in particular ways: understanding involves both recalling and relating ideas and acting upon them. This meaning of understanding is rather well expressed by Woods and Barrow (1975) as follows:

A man avers that he understands an argument in theoretical physics. He puts the argument into his own words, adduces concrete illustrations of the generalisations and abstractions in the argument, answers to my satisfaction all my questions relating to the argument, draws forth further consequences from aspects of the argument etc. This man is able to relate, in fact he *is* relating as he does all these things, as when he relates a generalisation or abstraction in the argument to specific concrete particulars.

It has been claimed (Davie, 1961) that the substitution of written

Figure 7.2: Henry VIII's Reign Seen as a Dialectic Evolution, Thesis and Antithesis being the Politics of the Tudor Dynasty and the Problems of Religion and Divorce, Respectively

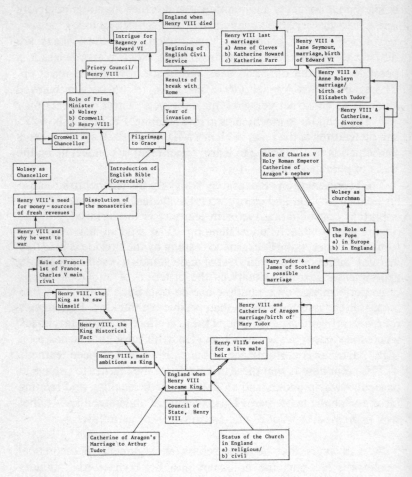

for oral examinations in the Scottish universities in the middle of the nineteenth century marked the weakening of reliable assessment of the understanding (as opposed to the knowledge) of the candidate. Tutorials on the one-to-one Oxbridge model may offer such possibilities, but economic constraints effectively rule them out in most universities.

Student Learning Strategies

Problem solving involves the following five steps: (1) decoding (comprehending) the problem; (2) selection of a likely hypothesis as a basis for a solution; (3) implementation (mentally, internally) of the hypothesis; (4) evaluation of the validity of the solution arrived at in step (3); and (5) reporting the solution to an external agent. In everyday learning the only public aspect of this process is at stage (5), but Pask and earlier Bruner (1956 and 1966) have been able to externalise step (3) by demonstrating the different strategies on which hypotheses are formulated.

The distinction between 'strategy' and 'style' is not clear cut as Cashdan (OU, 1971) has pointed out. Entwistle *et al.* (1978a) define a strategy as 'a description of the way a student *chooses* to tackle a specific learning task in the light of its perceived demands', whereas they see a style as 'a student's preferred way of tackling learning tasks generally'. The suggestion that strategies are more flexible and modifiable than styles is confirmed by Messick (1976). He describes styles as 'habitual modes of information processing' linked to basic personality and cognitive structure, and hence not susceptible to modification, whereas strategies are more specific and flexible, reflecting 'task requirement, problem content and situational constraints'. Cognitive styles and individual abilities affect the selection and organisation of cognitive strategies, but the particular strategy adopted will depend on the nature of the task.

Pask has identified two learning strategies from the way students set about learning the taxonomies of two 'charm-laden though grotesque' species of imaginary Martian fauna, the Clobbits and the Gandlemüller. The complexity of the learning task he devised is obvious from the following description of the Clobbits.

There are 10 subspecies of 'Clobbit' with two main subtypes, 'Clobs' and 'Bits'. There are 9 test boxes or branches in the classification tree and 7 physical characteristics are tested to make the requisite distinctions. For parts of the taxonomy, the values of other physical characteristics discriminate the classes equally well. The structure contains symmetries (for example, four 4-legged Bits and four 3-legged Bits); it also contains asymmetries (for example, the 4-legged Bits are first assigned to two subspecies by leg position); the 3-legged Bits are assigned by leg position to two subsets each containing two subspecies. Some of the names of the animals are assigned rationally (T stands for Triped; K stands for legs at corners, but since TK is used only for 3-legged creatures the suffix TK is redundant). Some names have no rational justification. There is background information about the behaviour and habitat of the Clobbits, some of which is relevant to the distinctions made (and might be used to make them redundant) and some of which is irrelevant. Finally, each subspecies of Clobbit is associated with a picture of one member of it. (Pask, 1975)

In one experiment (Pask, 1975), sixteen student subjects first read an introductory summary and then spent twenty-five minutes with cards which described the taxonomy, and which were arranged face downwards in five columns. The ten cards in the first column showed pictures of Clobbits; other cards described appearance, behaviour, code names and their derivation. The cards are reproduced in Holloway (1978).

Subjects were aware that some of the information was irrelevant, and that the taxonomy might be learned from data in only one or two of the columns. Cards could be examined in any order, one at a time, provided the subject indicated the questions he was asking himself and the hypotheses he was posing in choosing each one. Comments were recorded, as well as the order in which cards were examined and any notes (new cards) which the subject wrote. After taking a 30 item multiple choice test (80 per cent factual knowledge, 20 per cent ability to generalise) subjects were placed in an 'effective' or 'ineffective' teachback situation. (In the 'ineffective' situation errors were left uncorrected.) They then took the test again two weeks later at the start of a second session.

Pask found that in this free learning situation students adopted different strategies in learning the taxonomy. 'Serialists' learned in a step-by-step fashion, advancing simple hypotheses, and concentrating on one feature of the task at a time; 'holists' based their selection of cards on more complex 'multiple predicate' hypotheses — testing differences between animals on several counts, such as number of legs, mating behaviour and habitat.

The next step in the research design was to test the importance of relating teaching method to learning style. The students were set to learn the Gandlemüller taxonomy from linear programmes which had been designed to suit each type of learner. The serialist programme had 11 information and test frames while the holist programme had 25. The serialist programme included specific facts about low level concepts, while the holist programme introduced a range of facts at various levels, with information about overall task structure provided early on. In addition, the kind of information was also different: the holists were given more information not *strictly* relevant to the task in hand, including more diagrams, etc. Both matching and mismatching (e.g. serialists learning the holist programme) were introduced. Subjects were required to work through the programme until all wrong responses had been eliminated. This took up to one hour and was followed by another 30 item test which, on this occasion, provided information both on what was remembered and how it had been learned.

The research design and the results obtained showed that effective teachback and matching produced effective learning for students in each strategy, while mismatching had quite disastrous results. Pask (1975) concluded 'that the rate, quality and durability of learning is crucially dependent upon whether or not the teaching strategy is of a sort that suits the individual'.

Pask has also demonstrated these differences on computer displays on three artificial learning environments — CASTE (Course Assembly System and Tutorial Environment), Intuition (a portable version) and Thoughtsticker, a more flexible epistemological laboratory (Pask *et al.*, 1977) made up of computer programmes, associated autonomous microprocessors and graphics facilities, which allow the student freedom to interact with topics set for learning and to develop personal hierarchies of concept relationships.

In one study (Pask, 1975) innumerate, paid volunteers recruited from technical and art school and 'café society in Richmond and its neighbourhood' were set to learn statistics and probability theory. The subject matter had been arranged in a complex entailment structure which was visually displayed as in Figure 7.1. Key or 'Head' ideas had to be approached via their logically prior concepts, but the entailment structures reflected all the conceivable ways in which the content could be taught, and students were therefore free to choose their own route through the material. The students' learning track was lighted up on the computer display rather like a destination map on the Paris Metro, and each time a key idea had been 'understood' (i.e. derived by an acceptable route and correctly 'modelled' in performance terms on STATLIB, a modelling and simulation facility) a steady green lamp signalled success.

Inspection of the learning maps of different students confirmed the holist and serialist distinction. Holists began work on a second or third idea before mastering the first; serialists worked their way steadily up from one point in the taxonomy and did not explore other topics. Students adopted the same strategy across tasks. Robertson (1978), who describes what are basically the same phenomena as 'broad' and 'narrow' strategies, reported correlations of 0.85.

It is not being suggested that holists are 'good' learners and serialists 'poor' learners: in fact both reached the common goal with equal success. Their paths to that goal were, however, strikingly different. So, too, was their recall. Serialists remembered in 'string-like cognitive structures' in the sequence in which they had learned. They became confused when too many ideas were presented at once.

Holists learned, remembered and recapitulated as a whole: their accounts of their learning were much fuller and less programme-bound. They also made a higher number of inferential and irrelevant statements. Holists 'image an entire system of facts or principles', but some (irredundant holists) include only relevant and essential images, while others (redundant holists) 'entertain images that contain logically irrelevant or overspecific material, commonly derived from data used to "enrich" the curriculum, and the salient facts and principles are embedded in a network of redundant items' (Pask, 1975). Such redundancy may be of psychological importance for the redundant holist, since the images may serve 'to access, retain and manipulate whatever he was originally requested to learn'.

The difference between serialists and holists stands out rather clearly from the following teachback protocols where first a serialist and then a holist describe what they had discovered about the Gandlemüllers:

Zoologists have classified the Gandlemüller on the basis of physical characteristics. The three main types are Gandlers, Plongers, and Gandleplongers. Gandlers have no sprongs. Gandleplongers have one sprong. There are four sub-species of Gandler: M1, M2, B1, and B2. The Ms have one body, the Bs have two bodies. The M1 and B1 have a single cranial mound. The M2 and B2 have a double cranial mound. . .

Contrast this with the cavalier approach of the holist:

> I want to tell you about a funny Martian animal which has been recently discovered and classified by scientists conducting surveys. They are funny slug-like things with various protuberances. These animals are called Gandlemüllers, because they churn about in the swamps near the Equator and Gandle is Martian for swampmud, hence swampmudmiller. [Müller is German for miller.] These things churn through the mud eating it by some curious process which means they eat and excrete at the same time. . .

Operation and Comprehension Learning Styles and Versatility

The distinction between serialists and holists is based on how students tackle assignments in contrived learning situations where they have freedom to choose how they will learn. These strategies reflect broader 'operational' and 'comprehension' learning styles: 'operation learning' is Pask's term for that aspect of learning concerned with the mastery of procedural details, while 'comprehension learning' is concerned with 'building descriptions of what may be known' (Pask *et al.*, 1977). Operation learners 'pick up rules, methods and details, but may not see the subject as a whole' (Pask, 1976b); comprehension learners 'see the topic as a whole, and can describe the relationship between aspects of a topic' and re-interpret what they learn in their own terms. An appropriate blend of both styles is required if the student is to reach understanding on everyday learning tasks: students who achieve such a blend are described by Pask as 'versatile'. Bias to one or other style results in an incomplete approach to learning, and hence a pathology.

The comprehension learner's capacity to make connections within the subject matter, and beyond it, is a distinctive feature of his learning style. But the nature of the analogies he draws may be helpful for learning or merely self-indulgent. 'Valid' analogies are based on common principles, such as scientific laws, and involve correspondences between subordinate topics. The principle of simple oscillation, for example, can be defined in terms of friction and resistance, whether the oscillator is driven by machine or electricity, and an analogy which links these concepts would be regarded as 'valid'. 'Vacuous' analogies lack these correspondences, or at least the student cannot identify them.

Comprehension learners are prone to the pathology of 'globetrotting' — 'the misunderstanding of valid analogies, the use of vacuous analogies, or both' (Pask, 1976b). Entwistle (1978) defines globe-trotting as the 'search for interconnections and a broad overview, without supporting arguments or evidence'. Globetrotters indulge in speculation or broad generalisation without taking the trouble to master detail. Operational learners, on the other hand, rarely consider the possibility of linking up ideas: they are guilty of 'improvidence' — 'failure to use valid analogies, failure to use a common principle, or both' (Pask, 1976b). In short, they may fail to understand the overall significance of the learning task, or to move beyond factual details to their meaning.

In stringently controlled learning situations (Pask, 1976b) the pathologies occur less often. It is easy to see why. In teachback the student is forced both to recall what he has been reading and, in reteaching, to think through its meaning, answer questions, think up examples, and in short display 'understanding' in the terms which Woods and Barrow described earlier. A critical audience, like the expectation of assessment, keeps the lecturer, and the student, on his toes.

Pask is not a good communicator and anyone who seeks clarification from his published work may find it difficult. Fortunately Daniel (1975), Entwistle (1978) and Holloway (1978) have provided lucid manuals. But what does this strategy-style distinction boil down to? One way of clarifying it is in terms of what are, hopefully, valid analogies! Let us consider the reporting of a football match. In a newspaper like the *Guardian*, the report is generally abstract and interpretative: the grand strategy is described in terms of 'key incidents' or turning points which shape the flow of events; a report in the *Sunday Post*, on the other hand, is usually in terms of who did what to whom in which minute, and records specific free kicks, saves and passbacks. As accounts of the same game, they may be virtually unrecognisable: the former draws analogies beyond the immediate step-by-step events, while the latter describes the game almost solely in terms of what literally happened. Consider, too, that a holist might describe a play in terms of its general theme or message (*Macbeth* is about ambition and its consequences), whereas a serialist might see it in terms of its characters and the development of the plot without being aware of its underlying theme. Finally, the distinction might be conceived in terms of the recipe and the cake: the operationalist describes the cake in terms of how the ingredients are mixed and baked, but fails to see the finished product as anything but 'a cake'; the comprehension learner focuses on the cake as a work of art, indulges in fantasies about patisseries and the French way of life, and cannot tell you the recipe.

Both accounts are, of course, valid. W.B. Yeats perhaps summed up these complementary perspectives most tellingly in his poem 'Among School Children':

> O body swayed to music, O brightening glance
> How can we know the dancer from the dance? (Yeats, 1955)

Both kinds of knowledge are required for 'understanding', but only in stringently defined learning situations is the student *required* to combine his operation and comprehension learning.

The Spy Ring History Test

The Spy Ring History Test, and its parallel form, the Smugglers' Test, were devised to provide shorter and more exact measures of learning styles as well as a score of versatility. The SRHT takes between one and two hours, and involves memorising the names of agents and the history of a spy ring in three imaginary countries (Ruritania, Dionysia and Olympia) over five-year periods between 1880 and 1900. Paired associate lists of spy names indicate the channels of communication.

Success on the test depends on the individual's capacity to cope with comprehension questions ('What went wrong with the spy system around 1885?'), operation questions ('How could Abel communicate with Boris in 1890; by how many paths; what are they?'), and to display versatility by being able to predict a plausible next stage in the spy ring's history: 'a good prediction requires an appreciation of the symmetries and asymmetries in the network patterns as a cycle of changes (comprehension learning) and a mastery of the roles and rules that form a representative sequence of messages actually transmitted from one spy to another (operation learning)' (Pask *et al.*, 1977).

Early results on the SRHT are disappointing but interesting. Laurillard (1978) found that 24 out of 31 technology students had similar operation and comprehension scores, but high scorers on both were not necessarily 'versatile' (V), nor were biased students necessarily low on V. She suggested that V was perhaps more a measure of independent or productive (P) thinking, the capacity to go 'beyond the information given'. She rescored SRHT to distinguish memory items from measures of P and concluded that students with poor memories tended to be ineffective productive thinkers. Her other findings raise more doubts about the validity of SRHT: even the most successful students admitted to being confused by the instructions and working under severe time constraints: their success appeared to have been due in some part to imaginative and lucky guessing. Laurillard concluded that it would be unwise to predict a student's normal learning capabilities on the basis of V or P scores.

Learning to Learn

Pask (1976b) has reported some limited research on learning to learn. The most interesting study involved 24 sixth form and college of education students and extended over 5 two-hour sessions. Subjects were put in the situation of a student who has missed a lecture course and has two hours to prepare for an explanation/essay-type examination, based on set materials.

These consisted of a collection of papers by authors such as Jung, Kelly and Wittgenstein and, of course, represented more than could be mastered in the time available. Just before the examination a sheet with 35 salient topics, arranged in a ring, was presented and the subjects had to indicate which they felt confident they could answer and which they definitely could not. They were also invited to 'connect up' topics which they saw as going together to form an associative network.

The second (and possibly the third) session was devoted to study of the computer processed graphics of the students' associative networks, and to training in study methods. Students were taught simple principles of subject matter structure and how to reach 'understanding' and avoid 'globetrotting'. The fourth session was a repeat of the first with a new learning task, and the final session centred on discussion of associative networks. The SRHT provided information on learning style. Improvements were reported in examination achievement, the number of topics noted as being understood, and the complexity of the associative nets produced.

Trials with a control group pointed to the importance of training sessions for improving learning and increasing the structural complexity of the associative networks. But the results revealed important individual differences in response to this kind of help. Eight 'versatile' students had a high score on both learning tasks, while three students actually had lower scores and formed less complex networks on the second occasion. These students had low versatility and appeared to be operation learners. Further evidence is required before we can accept Pask's conclusion that 'it is possible, with a few exceptions, to teach students to learn more effectively by the application of sophisticated principles of learning' (Pask, 1976b).

Laurillard (1978) explored the relevance of Pask's styles of learning to students' accounts of subject matter they were currently studying. She gave each 20 minutes to explain a topic to a naive interviewer; students were free to bring any notes they needed for their explanation. An analysis of the recorded teachback protocols for three topics (equilibrium diagrams (9 students), reaction kinetics (8) and stereographic projection (8)) is reported. Although the circumstances in which topics were being studied were subsequently explored, unfortunately no questions appear to have been asked about how the students prepared for this teachback situation.

Laurillard (1978) trained judges successfully to score the protocols on the following criteria of operation and comprehension learning.

Operation learning (procedure building)
O1   uses definitions
O2   uses procedural or relational rules
O3   makes logical derivations
Comprehension learning (description building)
C1   compares or distinguishes theory and practice
C2   interprets theory in terms of, or refers to, the real world
C3   introduces (strictly) redundant or irrelevant information
C4   compares two or more situations (e.g. finds an analogy) or considers a simplified situation

She found students exhibited contrasting styles of explaining but bias to comprehension or operation learning differed from topic to topic. No student was consistently heavily biased in one direction, although the greater openness of the teachback situation, compared with SRHT, provided more opportunities for students to exhibit bias.

In the following example, which is scored on the above criteria, two students display different bias in explaining the interpretation of equilibrium diagrams in metallagraphy.

David:

02   'Well basically you find alloy 1, so you follow that line and you've got temperature up here, you've got element A on this
01   side, element B on this side. There's percentage weights of these along the X axis. . . What you have to do is, there's a rule that says that when you go across a solid section of a phase diagram — which is this bottom half, the top half is liquid.
01   You go from single phase to double phase to single phase to double phase across the bottom of the diagram. The loops here between the solid phase and the liquid phase is
C2   compositions of liquid and solid. It takes some time to cool down, and solid's formed through that cooling range because you have two different elements at different melting points. . .'

George:

   'Well, basically this is an equilibrium diagram taken of an alloy. At one end of the diagram we have pure metal A, where
O1   pure metal B is at the other end, so you've got mixtures, i.e. alloys between that point in different proportions. These dia-
C3   grams were made by people who were very dedicated, sitting in little attics and things years ago, by doing cooling curves on certain metals, in alloys, in certain proportions, noting from the liquid phase what happened as the metal cooled down. They would note the temperature at which the solid would start to appear, and then the solid would be with the liquid then for a certain temperature range, then at the end of that temperature range, there would be all solid, and that tempera-
C2   ture too was noted, and it would cool right down to purely solid. Then a lot of these were plotted, all the way across and this would give a graph from all the different points. . .'

Laurillard observes: 'the second student never got around to explaining the actual procedure used in equilibrium diagrams; the first student explained nothing but procedure'. The significant point, however, is that neither student had shown a strong bias towards either type of learning on the SRHT.

Conclusion

It is not within the competence of the present writer to do justice to the many facets of Pask's work on learning. What can be said, however, is that he has exteriorised different strategies by which students approach learning tasks and shown how matching of teaching method to preferred strategy results in highly successful learning. Another point is that stringent performance and teachback criteria have been shown to promote learning, and this appears to be because they force students to articulate a response which involves blending the contributions from different learning styles. Admittedly the samples are small and not entirely representative, but these results would appear to be well established.

Entwistle (1978) has suggested that Pask's account of learning may only be applicable to the sciences. It is true that the subject matter of the sciences can most helpfully and convincingly be represented in entailment structures, but that is not to say that topics in history, literature, philosophy or psychology cannot be studied on a serialist model. A student set to write an essay on an abstract topic may, indeed will, require to develop analytical skills to elucidate complex ideas and to explore the relationships and sequencing of the subject; indeed, it may be the case that all subjects can be approached on a step-by-step basis, at least at one level. What does spring to mind, however, is the relationship between the strategies in everyday learning situations. An effective learner, such as a successful advocate, a top civil servant or an academic, has qualities of perseverance which may cause him to think through a topic he has made sense of initially on a serialist/operation model. It is hard to disagree with Laurillard's (1978) conclusion that it is the context of learning which determines the degree of mastery attained: but this is simply putting Pask's point about versatility in another way. Failure to learn may be defined as the point at which one stops trying: pressure to express himself in writing, or verbally, or by demonstrating a skill will lead the serialist to generalise. But as Robertson (1978) has suggested, differences in the capacity to do so may reflect verbal or spatial ability rather than cognitive style.

Pask's findings appear to have direct implications for teaching methods. The case for experimenting with matching hardly needs to be argued, although there are many practical and theoretical problems which will be discussed in Chapter 8. His findings provide a clue to the explanation of differential ratings of lecturers by students. With regard to textbooks, too, there is a strong case for prescribing a wide range from which students might select. Perhaps the main implication would be most difficult to implement: staff should spend more time providing students with opportunities for effective teachback. Peer teaching could make a valuable contribution here which would not be perceived as threatening by students.

A final point relates to the extent to which strategies and styles are modifiable. Strategies appear to be consistent across tasks. Bruner (1956) was able to train children to develop more sophisticated strategies for tackling simple classification tasks, but with more complex materials, such as the taxonomies, one wonders how far students can be trained to adopt strategies different from those they naturally incline to. Messick (1976) suggests that students may be more or less conscious of the strategies available to them: it may be possible to train them 'to use optimal problem-solving and learning strategies consistent with their cognitive styles, and even to learn to shift to less congenial strategies that are more effective for a particular task than are their preferred ones'. The evidence on matching teaching to learning, on teachback, and on 'learning to learn' does suggest that students can be helped to develop more effective strategies which help them to think through their learning. The limits to that help may, however, be set by the individual's learning style whose origins reach deep into the basic structures and formative experiences of the personality and which may be less susceptible to change.

8 LEARNING AND COGNITIVE STYLE

When I was looking for a research topic for my MEd thesis, I went for advice to one of the senior psychology lecturers. We had a short discussion and then he formulated a penetrating question, 'Are you basically a cautious, play-it-safe type of person, or do you like to take risks?' When I mention that I went on to do a thesis on the history of teacher training in Scotland between 1906 and 1939 readers will gather the answer I gave.

Psychologists like to put people into categories on the basis of their answers to such questions. One of the best-known distinctions is that between extraverts and introverts. The assumption is that there is a 'core' personality consisting of stable, persisting traits which can be measured. The concept of cognitive style summarises and links up different features of personality and attitude: Messick (1976) defines cognitive style as 'high level heuristics that organise and control behaviour across a wide variety of situations'. It functions as a 'tracer element' distinguishing between attitudes, temperament and motivation of different people. It is assumed, for example, that the student with an authoritarian personality, with its tendency to rigidity, inflexibility and ethnocentricism, would be likely to perceive issues in single-minded, dualistic terms, and this might affect his capacity to think flexibly about issues encountered in his academic work and to solve problems.

Cognitive styles purport to be bipolar with regard to level, neutral in value and universal rather than field specific. They differ from measures of intellectual abilities in that they describe *how* an individual tackles a task, i.e. acquires, stores, retrieves and transforms information, rather than how *well* he tackles it, with the overtones of success and failure. The bipolar nature of cognitive styles means that each end of the continuum is held to reflect characteristic strengths and weaknesses which reflect the functioning of the core personality. The expression of cognitive style is reflected in the choice of specialist field of study (arts and science) and preference for teaching method: students with differing cognitive styles may have different needs for structure and may thrive in different teacher-student environments. Cognitive style may also be related to student performance; inappropriate 'matching' of style with area of study may lead to underachievement, or transfer to more compatible academic fields.

In this chapter I want to review evidence on two cognitive styles, Witkin's field dependence (fd) and field independence (fi) and Hudson's convergence-divergence dimensions. The latter I shall discuss in the context of the distinction that has been drawn between students who are described as 'syllabus bound' (sylbs) and 'syllabus free' (sylfs).

Before embarking on this, however, certain caveats are in order. Typically dimensions of cognitive style are based on results obtained from performance testing or questionnaire responses on a personality or attitude inventory. The former are, of course, more 'objective' than the latter in that they indicate what the student *can* do, as opposed to what he says he *will* do. But on both measures the results for the majority of students are likely to be distributed normally about the mean and any score above or below it will merely indicate a *tendency* towards one or other end of the continuum in question. Thus the dichotomy of the extraversion-introversion dimension, which usually is made about the mid-point of the distribution on the Eysenck Personality Inventory, will result in the identification of many 'extraverts', only very few of whom will have extreme scores. To describe an individual who just falls within a category in terms of the extremes of that category is therefore to oversimplify and indeed to distort reality. Moreover, the scores, and the categorisation, are not particularly reliable and clinically would be treated with great caution.

A further point should be borne in mind. It is self-evident that the individual's perception of the context will have an important influence on how he behaves. Any group of students meeting in tutorial for the first time will relax only slowly, as people size each other up. Common experience leads to the development of a group culture, and role differentiation occurs. The way roles are played will reflect the core personality as it finds expression within that group. Students, like teachers, 'bend and flex' to the situation they find themselves in, the role they are expected to play, and the role they find congenial. First year tutorial groups are notoriously tongue-tied, although outside the classroom individuals may be articulate enough. Indeed, some of the students are likely to be 'extraverts' on a paper-and-pencil test, but that does not mean they behave in a recognisably extravert way in the tutorial situation.

So, too, with motivation. It is often suggested that students can be grouped into two categories: those who study for intrinsic reasons (interest in the subject itself) and those who study for extrinsic reasons (career and financial advantage of a degree qualification). Again the proportion of students at the extremes may be quite small: it is more likely that some aspects of some courses hold or evoke intrinsic appeal for many students,within the wider perspective of the recognised extrinsic advantages of securing a degree.

Most people are somewhere 'in the middle' with regard to any particular measure or trait. There is a danger that labels which conveniently summarise the extremes of dimensions, which are themselves psychological artefacts, may be attached to individuals rather than to particular behaviours which, in certain circumstances, individuals may manifest. So despite my response to my psychology tutor I would still maintain that, in the right circumstances, I would not be afraid to draw bow at a venture: how else would I ever have married?

Cognitive Style: Nineteen Varieties

At least 19 cognitive styles have been identified (Messick, 1976). In addition to field dependence-independence and convergence-divergence, they include levelling and sharpening, reflection and impulsivity, compartmentalisation (rigid versus flexible), cognitive complexity versus simplicity and risk-taking versus cautiousness. The problem is that there are many plausible ways of conceptualising individual differences: Bruner (1956), for example, suggested that one important distinction was between people who could do only one thing at a time and those who could do several. Lewis (1976) makes the point that it is important to identify the one or two dimensions (if such exist) which really do summarise, and better still explain, major differences in the way students learn.

Kogan (1976) has suggested that cognitive styles may be classified in terms of their distance from the ability domain. Some, such as field independence, are assessed on a performance dimension, others, such as convergence, imply value distinctions, while still others imply purely stylistic differences.

Before proceeding to discuss the dimensions of field dependence and convergence, a brief note is provided about the styles of reflection –impulsivity and levellers and sharpeners which appear to have relevance for student learning.

Research on reflection has been reported only with elementary schoolchildren by Kagan (1966). Reflectives have a high desire to be correct on tests which involve matching figures, and are willing to tolerate ambiguity and to suspend judgements in the course of securing the 'correct' answer. Impulsives on the other hand blurt out answers, jumping to the first conclusion as the correct one. Their response time is faster, but their accuracy is much lower. Boys tend to be more reflective than girls. High reflectivity appears to be associated with high performance in mathematics, but is a disadvantage in visual arts, humanities and the social sciences.

Gardner and his colleagues (1959) have suggested that people can be differentiated on the basis of how they recall events such as stories, jokes, incidents, etc. 'Levellers' tend to simplify in retelling by omitting inconsistencies and condensing elements; it is suggested that this occurs at the time of registering the information by a process of 'fusion' of the different elements as they are assimilated into the memory store. 'Sharpeners', on the other hand, recall vividly, but detail in the story may be exaggerated to such an extent that the total structure may come to be distorted. Evidence from recall of the story of the Pied Piper by 41 female college students (aged 18 to 22) is provided in Holzman and Gardner (1972). The findings suggest that women are more prone to be levellers than men.

It is possible that both of these cognitive styles may have relevance for the way students learn and recall, but direct evidence is required.

Field Dependence and Field Independence

The late Herman Witkin and his colleagues have published voluminously on the field dependence (fd) and field independence (fi) dimensions over the past 30 years. Several recent articles (Witkin, 1971; Witkin *et al.*, 1977c; Witkin and Goodenough, 1977b; Witkin, Goodenough and Oltman, 1977a) summarise the current state of the research.

Witkin was concerned with the general issue of psychological differentiation. The early experiments on perception have been widely described (e.g. Open University Course E281, 1971) and consist of a rod and frame test and a body adjustment test. In the latter a subject, seated within a small tilted room, is required to adjust his body to the upright from an initially tilted position. Some subjects take their cue from the surrounding field, others are largely independent of it. Thus, when actually sitting at an angle of up to 30 degrees, and aligned to the room field dependants will report that they are sitting perfectly straight. Field independants show greater autonomy in their ability to adjust their body to the upright, regardless of the orientation of the room. A paper-and-pencil embedded-figures test was subsequently developed in which the subject is required to separate figure from ground in the study of patterns. Results on the three tests intercorrelate highly: 'the common denominator underlying individual differences in performance in all these tasks is the extent to which a person is able to deal with a part of a field separately from the field as a whole' (Witkin, 1971).

Further research suggested to Witkin that the fi-fd continuum underlay a still broader dimension involving both analysis and restructuring in intellectual and perceptual activities, and it is to this that Witkin refers when he writes of 'global' and 'articulated' cognitive styles. The features of the 'articulated' or differentiated style (Witkin, Goodenough and Oltman, 1977a) include: (a) cognitive ability to organise unstructured fields and to experience parts of organised fields as discrete; (b) sense of separate identity, including awareness of one's own needs and values and autonomy in personal functioning; (c) a greater awareness of the body as having definite limits or boundaries and of structure between discrete yet interrelated parts; and (d) control over impulse expression and use of specialised defences (e.g. projecton, intellectualisation) as opposed to blanket defences (e.g. repression) for dealing with the consequences of potentially disturbing experiences. Research findings suggest that these traits, which refer to the *process* of knowing and relating, develop up to the age of 17 and thereafter are stable. Witkin and Goodenough (1977b) currently define the fd-fi dimension as 'extent of autonomy of external referents' and now conceive of it as a value neutral cognitive style, located within a domain of 'self-nonself segregation', which is one of three indicators of the general concept of differentiation.

Witkin's work has been criticised, for example by Vernon (1969), for failing to provide adequate norms for instruments such as the Embedded Figures Test. He has suggested that the fd-fi dimension is simply 'spatial ability' under a new name and this would explain the sex differences consistently found, girls being more fd. Correlations are certainly higher with scores on mathematical aptitude than verbal tests, and there are high correlations, too, with the analytical cluster of scales (e.g. block formation) on intelligence tests such as the WAIS (Wechsler Adult Intelligence Scale). But even if these and other criticisms, such as the need to control for social class, are substantiated, the dimension is still of considerable interest because of the way it relates individual characteristics to the academic setting.

As suggested above, field dependants find difficulty in tackling tasks which are presumed to involve a capacity to restructure. Examples are achieving alternative perspectives in spatial visualisation tasks, or breaking free of an induced mental 'set' in problem solving. Thus they work from each example in a sequence in turn rather than developing hypotheses through which to explain the underlying concept, and this step-by-step approach is reflected in a learning curve which shows gradual improvement. There is some, though not conclusive, evidence that they have the same difficulty with tactile and auditory tasks, such as identifying theme tunes in a musical arrangement. On the other hand, fd's are skilled in social relationships. They are sensitive, although this depends on the situation. Witkin emphasises these strengths of the fd end of the continuum to illustrate the value-free nature of the dimension. By contrast, fi's have a highly developed capacity to restructure cognitively: they can impose their own structures on a field or, within a field, construct alternative structures. In problem solving, for example, they develop hypotheses on the basis of each encounter with successive examples: they impose structure on the learning task by extracting general principles relevant to the data, and concept acquisition appears to occur after several trials by a kind of flash of insight. They are more analytical and carry a more differentiated or articulated frame of reality than field dependants. On the other hand, they are relatively deficient in social skills, being regarded as impersonal, cold and distant.

One longitudinal study of students in higher education (Witkin *et al.*, 1977c) confirmed that score on the dimension has almost no relationship to overall academic performance and a low correlation with conventional aptitude tests. On the other hand, fi's are likely to do better than fd's in subjects such as mathematics, where problem solving involves 'taking some critical element out of the context in which it is presented and restructuring the problem material so that the element is now used in a different way' (Witkin, 1971). Similar findings have also been reported in the sciences, engineering and architecture. In some education courses (Witkin *et al.*, 1977c) fd's do best, but general evidence for their high achievement is as yet rather limited 'because evidence on the social sensitivity and social skills of fd people has only recently emerged'.

Cognitive style is predictive of initial choice and persistence in academic subject and career choice, and has implications for teaching methods. Fi's tend to choose subjects where analytical skills are called for (e.g. physical and biological sciences, maths, engineering, etc.) and to enter related occupations; fd's choose social sciences and humanities. But choice of subject is influenced by many factors including social expectations, occupational prospects, etc., and there is evidence that students move away from fields which are incompatible with their cognitive styles towards more congenial specialisms. Thus, within science, fi's are likely to be persisters, while fd's will transfer to courses in arts and social science; traffic in the other direction is likely to be lighter, partly because of the inherent difficulties of qualifications and course requirements, but also because of the 'broad gauge' nature of the arts and social science field. A subject like psychology, for example, has both a 'hard' scientific 'end' (in experimental psychology) and a 'softer' human end in clinical or social psychology, so that all students can find a niche congenial to their cognitive style.

Cognitive style has implications both for what students learn and how they should be taught. Fd's pay more attention to social materials and learn and remember them better; they are also more susceptible to external motivation and sensitive to personal criticism; they find it difficult to structure material, but can learn materials which are highly structured, such as programmed learning, as effectively as fi's; they tend to pay attention to the salient cues in a learning situation and may neglect the less salient, and, as suggested above, they adopt passive as opposed to active learning strategies.

Some investigations of teachers who are fd and fi have been carried out, to see if their style affects their teaching behaviours; a related question has also been considered, namely the benefits and problems in seeking to match styles of teachers and students. The evidence so far collected has been from questionnaire studies rather than direct observation, and the findings (Witkin *et al.*, 1977c) are rather tentative. Fds' social orientation leads them to favour discussion methods and to allow students a greater role in structuring the learning situation; they give less negative evaluation to pupils, a finding consistent with their greater reliance on others for self-definition and their consequent need to maintain good relationships. Fi's, on the other hand, emphasise structure in their teaching, even in 'discovery' situations, make many references to standards, and criticise pupils. They are seen to teach principles, whereas fd's are more often viewed as teachers of 'facts', but both groups of teachers are viewed as equally competent.

'Match' is important only if it can be shown to affect the quality of learning. The evidence is not conclusive. It is likely that teachers and students of similar cognitive styles would be mutually attracted to each other; but the case for mismatching can also be argued: fi teachers of maths would be likely to help fd's by imposing greater structure through their teaching. Of course teachers respond differently to different students: studies of therapy sessions suggest that therapists intervene significantly more often with fd patients than with fi's, asking the latter more open-ended questions and the former questions that are more structured. Therapists are also shown to favour supportive therapy with fd's and modifying forms of therapy with fi's. At the same time, there is a higher level of communication between patient and therapist when both are fd's: both have a mutual desire to seek agreement and reinforcement in the discussion situation. Although fd's are generally popular in some circumstances, such as sharing living accommodation and co-operative task performance, individuals may prefer to interact with others who are similar to them in cognitive style; under conditions of conflict, interpersonal attraction is low in groups composed of fi's.

Differentiation appears to be the product of both heredity and experiential factors. In part it is caused by segregation of neuro-physiological functions leading to greater lateral specialisation of the hemispheres of the brain (Witkin *et al.*, 1977a). But 'overwhelming importance' is also attached to cross-cultural and other evidence on early upbringing. The qualities of fi are seen to be fostered where the mother adopts a role which stimulates the traits of dominance, independence and active striving. Witkin and Goodenough (1977b) suggest that people may be trained to become equally competent in the skills and competences of both ends of the fd-fi dimension. They designate students with access to only one of the styles as 'fixed', while students with access to both styles are 'mobile'. There does appear to be evidence that competence in restructuring skills, such as disembedding, can be developed; further research into programmes which will enhance interpersonal skills is acknowledged to be necessary.

Although position on the fd-fi continuum is assessed quantitatively, the usefulness of the scale is qualitative: the research highlights important individual differences in perception which explain why students are likely to find certain fields of study congenial. Although students working within the subject area which matches their cognitive style do appear to have somewhat higher achievement than unmatched students, perhaps the more important contribution of the research to the study of academic performance is in helping to explain such factors as persistence, drop out and transfer.

But the link between cognitive style and strategies adopted with particular learning tasks remains to be forged. Most of the evidence on restructuring, for example, is based on laboratory experiments: the critical question is how far such everyday learning tasks as essay writing, project work and examination answering are differentially tackled by students with different styles. How does the greater restructuring capacity of the fi, for example, manifest itself?

The evidence seems fairly clear that the fd-fi dimension is spatial-visual and has particular relevance for explaining differences in problem solving ability in such fields as engineering, architecture and the sciences. Ability to differentiate and to restructure are, of course, equally important in other fields, as in the analysis of character in literature or in the exploration of value perspectives in education or sociology. In these fields students are expected to acquire skills similar to those displayed by Marton's 'depth' processors, but the fd student appears not to be endowed with them.

This example perhaps highlights the slippery nature of the concept of cognitive style. After all, 'capacity to restructure' is simply a grandiose way of describing insightful behaviour, which in turn implies a certain capacity for divergent or creative behaviour. Is field independence, then, a separate or overlapping dimension? Messick's (1976) projected factor analytic study of the items of scales currently in use may help to answer that question.

Sylbs and Sylfs

All students are likely to appreciate a clearly defined academic framework which provides guidelines about course objectives, set work and assessment. It has been suggested, however, that some students are 'syllabus bound' (sylbs) in the sense that they work happily within the confines and structure of the framework while others, who are 'syllabus free' (sylfs), treat it as a point of departure or as a curb to their wide ranging intellectual interests. In this section we shall look at the characteristics and correlates of sylbs and sylfs and seek to explore both the origins of these attitudes to the curriculum and the implications for study behaviour.

Studies reviewed earlier (e.g. Becker, 1961; Snyder, 1971) have described the academic pressures to which many students are subjected. Time spent in class is higher in such structured fields as medicine, science and technology (Wilson, 1978a), since competence on the course requires mastery of basic material. These subject areas are consequently likely to prove more attractive to students who prefer structure. In other fields, particularly in arts and social science, curricula can reflect the personal interest of staff and students to a much greater degree, although the scope for individual choice will exist within a framework of compulsion. Thus essay topics and options are chosen by the student but normally from within a prescribed range. The opportunities for the student to plan his own course of study are very limited, at least in British higher education (Percy and Ramsden, 1980).

Sylbs are likely to be much less adventurous in their approach to study than sylfs. Parlett, who operationalised the dimension in a study at MIT, found that they would endorse such statements as 'I usually only study what I am required to study', and 'I prefer not to be left to work in my own way as I get nothing done', while rejecting statements like 'I am often involved in following up my own ideas when I am supposed to be doing homework', and 'I have several well-developed intellectual interests outside my school work'. The sylb then takes a more restricted and conventional view of what he must study: it is tempting to see him as the kind of student who looks for 'spoon feeding' and who infuriates his teacher by his 'what do I have to do to pass?' attitude. Safe, conformist, accepting, unadventurous, yet a sound and reliable enough worker within the clearly defined arrangements for the course. The sylf, on the other hand, is likely to have a quite different attitude to study. He finds the syllabus restricting, he challenges the ideas his teachers present, he has a wide range of outside intellectual interests which are absorbing and conflict with the demands of the set work. As one MIT student ruefully remarked, time spent on private interests was 'taken out of the time the Institute wants you to spend on your studies' (Parlett, 1970) and often at the expense of academic performance. Some students adopt cynical conforming attitudes at least in the short term; others retreat into their private world and find personal satisfaction which sustains them through routine academic exercises. Indeed it is the imaginative independence of the sylf that is most striking: in studies of creative scientists and architects, the qualities displayed by sylfs are those most associated with success.

Sylbs and sylfs actually behave differently in class. Parlett found that sylbs were good attenders, sat at the front of the class rather than the back, and did more homework than sylfs, but significantly they did less well on individual projects.

Parlett's syllabus-bound scale defined high scorers as sylbs and low scorers as sylfs. Entwistle and Wilson (1977), however, suggested that students may, in some cases, be both sylbs and sylfs. Where the course requirements are strongly defined they may be compelled to stay close to the syllabus, but they could still study in a sylf-like way. Such students might, like the 'cue-seeker', read up a few topics in depth and independently relate ideas from different parts of the subject and from their store of wider reading. In the Lancaster study, therefore, each dimension was assessed on a separate scale.

The dimensions do not correlate with measures of study methods which tap conscientiousness and being organised. Nor is there a strong direct relationship with academic performance, but Entwistle found that sylbs did well in honours English and that a low sylb score was predictive of degree preformance in history. Students in different fields of study do, however, score differently on these dimensions. Students of maths, engineering, chemistry and French scored higher mean sylb scores than expected, while students of English and sociology scored higher as sylfs. Historians stood out as a group who scored low on both dimensions, while honours French students were more syllabus bound and less syllabus free than expected. The group with the lowest sylf and highest sylb score was women who studied mathematics.

Parlett questions whether the sylb/sylf distinction points to a 'basic and long-standing psychological difference' between students, or whether it is simply 'a short-term disparity in styles of adaptation to the college environment'. In Chapter 3 we saw how students' interpretation of, and reaction to, the academic context reinforced conformist attitudes, although these often matched expectations laid down by the external examination system at school. Sylb-like behaviour might also be induced in first year students because of their lack of confidence in their abilities, the genuine difficulty of the material, reflecting school-college mismatch, and exacerbated, perhaps, by poor teaching, and even by an inadequate conception of the student role.

But more deep-seated differences in core personality structure may also account for these stylistic differences in attitude to study. There are many thought provoking parallels in the distinctions between different types of students made by Hudson (1966), Sofer (1961),

Asch (1955), Biggs (1978) and Witkin (1971). The basic questions to be answered are (a) the sources within the individual of 'sylb'– and 'sylf'–like behaviour, and (b) the implications for study methods, including the pathologies to which these approaches may give rise.

Hudson (1966 and 1968) has linked his work with 'convergers' and 'divergers' to 'sylbs' and 'sylfs', although he has pointed out that the terms are not synonymous. The basic distinction is well-known, being made on the basis of performance by sixth formers on objective tests of intelligence (the AH5) and open-ended tests such as the 'Use of Objects' where candidates have to write down as many uses as they can think of for a familiar object, such as a brick. On average, 30 per cent of pupils were defined as 'convergers', since they were good at objective items although they lacked fluency on open-ended questions, while the same percentage of pupils sharing the opposite characteristics were described as 'divergers'. Many of the latter appeared to have difficulty in following a pattern of precise, logical thought.

Convergers are like sylbs in that they enjoy the structured setting of the school and are more likely than divergers (in a ratio of 3:1) to choose subjects such as maths, physical science and classics where the subject matter is unambiguous. Divergers, on the other hand, found school boring and restricting: they were much more likely to study subjects on the arts side such as English, history and modern languages. Hudson is specially interested in the relationship between personality and subject choice, and in the images schoolboys hold of different occupations. Convergers are much more likely to become scientists, and they are very clear by adolescence that science involves a commitment to respect for conventional values, masculinity and self-control (as opposed to pleasure seeking). But the intriguing question is why certain pupils should be attracted to such a life style which, once embraced, confirms the underlying characteristics in the individual personality, while others adopt the warm, person-centred style of the artist.

It is possible that the basic differences between 'sylbs' and 'sylfs' lie in their attitude to authority and to their perception of themselves. The sylb, like the converger, appears to welcome authority, presumably because clearly defined situations provide emotional security: hence his desire to avoid the complex and ambiguous subject matter of human issues, and hence his relief at having a course outline which prescribes what he must study. The sylf, on the other hand, like the diverger, may perceive authority as posing a threat to his imaginative independence: he will prefer subject matter which allows him 'room to manoeuvre', and the study of human motives and behaviour allows him opportunities to work with stimulating, challenging subject matter in which a variety of interpretations may be advanced.

But it is likely that sylbs and sylfs also differ radically in self-image. Sylfs have striking independence of mind, wide-ranging interests, and the self-confidence to pursue their own ideas, even in the face of criticism and hostility. Their capacity to use ideas actively by making relationships, rather in the manner of Pask's 'holists', suggests that they have qualities of 'inner directedness' which make them more conscious of their drives and impulses and able to accept and direct them. By contrast the 'other directed' students in Sofer's study (i.e. those more susceptible to the influence of others and more reliant on guidance and direction) were likely to have a weak, immature and passive self-image, to be less aware of their own emotions and impulses, and so less able to differentiate between their own images and external factors such as group pressures and authoritative-sounding sources of influence. Sofer herself draws parallels between these findings and those in Asch's studies of perception, where 'yielders' were distinguished from 'independents' by their capacity for self-avoidance. 'Yielders' were those subjects who gave in to group pressure: 'independents', who resisted the group, were flexible, risk takers, prepared to try the novel and unexpected, and placed high value on creativity and independence.

Both Hudson and Sofer see the origins of these basic personality characteristics in the interaction between genetic endowment, temperament and early childhood experience. Freud claimed that those who repress fiercely will have poor access to 'primary process' thought, i.e. the stream of mental associations essential to imaginative thought. Interestingly enough, massive repression is also held to be a characteristic defence style of levellers. Hudson sees the traits of convergence and divergence as defence mechanisms: the converger opts to work with 'things' because he cannot cope with 'human' issues, the diverger finds authority threatening and seeks escape in 'human' subject matter. On the other hand, the 'other-directed' person has a much poorer attitude to himself than the inner-directed person, and is much less aware of his true inner feelings.

Sylbs and sylfs are likely to have characteristic approaches to study and corresponding pathologies, but these await confirmation by research. The greater independence of mind and self-confidence of the sylfs may mean that they adopt 'cue seeking' strategies so that the limited time and energy they have to spare for the course are put to good purpose, and it is tempting to see connections with holist and 'depth' strategies in the way they tackle assignments. At the same time, their style is likely to lead them into a pathology in which self-indulgence or dilettantism overwhelms their capacity to order their ideas and discipline their thinking. If globetrotting is to be avoided, the sylf must rein in his imaginative independence and systematise his thinking in a sustained manner.

The sylb accepts the department's or tutor's definition of the learning situation. It is likely, therefore, that he will perceive his learning task as that of imbibing conventional wisdom rather than challenging assumptions. This does not mean to say that he cannot be an effective student; but it is unlikely that he will be radical. Their suggestibility to influence may be discernible in tutorial discussion and in their difficulty in reconciling arguments based on different frameworks of values. The sylb's pathology is likely to be a passivity and dependence which invites spoon feeding; his dependence on externally imposed structure renders him less and less able to challenge the assumptions on which the structure is based; his efficiency at mastering the trees makes him incapable of seeing the wood. He generates 'cow' while the sylf produces 'bull'.

Sylbs and sylfs are, of course, two abstractions: students will tend to one or other style of behaving, depending on the context. Indeed, for the highest academic success both qualities may be said to be necessary. As McKellar (1957) (quoted in Fontana, 1977) puts it, 'holistic' or creative thinking is required 'to *author* any worthwhile creative act, while rational thinking is the *editor* who sifts through the ideas generated by "holistic" thinking, isolates those which are most relevant and puts them to use'.

Whatever the origins of sylb- and sylf-like behaviour, there would presumably be wide agreement that the imaginative independence of the sylf is a quality which should be developed in all students. Teaching methods, and the setting and marking of assignments, could perhaps play a role here. There is some evidence (Blis and Ogborn, 1977) that independent work and projects give students experiences which generate confidence and intrinsic motivation and encourage them to take greater responsibility for their own learning, while the work of Biggs (1973), to be reviewed in the next chapter, suggests that the ways in which grades from different parts of a course are combined can both stimulate and reward the independent learner. Briefly he distinguishes between a *union* model, where marks (e.g. for class work, objective tests and practical exercises) are simply added together, and a *disjunction* model, in which the best mark is taken from different aspects of the work (i.e. 'the student has to be good at one of several alternative things'). The union model, the most common, favours students who are class oriented and teacher dependent, who systematically schedule private work sessions and who rote learn significant detail, but who nevertheless try to interrelate their work, while the disjunction model operates against such students, but favours the 'loner' who gets deeply absorbed in particular aspects of the subject.

The two models are related to the question of whether in higher education it is better to promote 'breadth' or 'depth' student learning: 'union' and 'disjunctive' methods may be used to encourage different types of student study behaviour.

9 MODELS OF STUDENT LEARNING

In previous chapters I have reviewed empirical findings which have helped fill out our notion of how students learn in higher education. The discussion has centred on such themes as the context of learning, the general pattern of student intellectual and ethical development, the role of the peer group, and the approach, strategies and styles of thinking students display in learning complex material. One notable gap has been the omission of reference to the psychological literature on the intellectual, personality and motivational correlates of success and failure in higher education, but this may be excused since useful reviews (e.g. Entwistle and Wilson, 1977) already exist. Such factors as general ability, level of anxiety, introversion, and level and type of motivation, undoubtedly play an important part in performance. The relationship between these variables and academic success is not necessarily direct or linear, however, and it is to the interactions and clustering of the variables that we must look if we are to understand how students tackle particular learning tasks.

Analysis must lead to a new synthesis if we are to understand the significance of this considerable body of research evidence which touches on different aspects of student learning. The pieces of the jigsaw must be fitted together to recreate a reality which is both recognisable and also more meaningful, in the sense that it satisfyingly explains why students should study in the ways they do. In this chapter I want to review briefly five models of the process of student learning which have been advanced by researchers. The first is by Entwistle and Wilson (1977), the second is by Biggs (1978) who has reported a series of studies conducted in Australia over the past ten years, the third is by Entwistle, Hanley and Hounsell (1978a) based on their recent work, the fourth is by Laurillard (1978) whose research at the University of Surrey has previously been referred to, and the fifth is my own attempt to construct a developmental model of student learning.

A model is a simplification of reality; McLeish (1970) defines it as 'a scaled down representation of some object, process or concept'. Models can be useful in summarising and integrating knowledge and ideas within a field. Invariably a model reflects assumptions about the nature of the process being described; a model is likely to be incomplete in that not all the relevant factors in a situation may have been explored or even recognised. Partial and competing models may be better than no model at all: in our current state of knowledge about students and their characteristics, model making is like trying to fashion bricks without straw. Maturational data about students, for example, are totally lacking. Only the Americans, Perry and Heath, have looked at student development longitudinally, and that without reference to conventional academic performance. We lack any normative data on sylbs and sylfs, cue seekers and field dependants, and any indication of how these qualities develop and their link with academic performance. How far, for example, are the sylf's qualities of imaginative independence already present at entry to university, and how far does successful study at university confirm and develop them? And what do we mean by 'successful' study? Academic performance as conventionally assessed may be an inadequate criterion of the achievement of the intellectual goals of the university: or is it to be assumed that the distinction between classes of degree reflects the attainment of levels of thinking and understanding as well as knowledge and skills? And does this hold across types of institution in higher education and different fields of study?

Even if we lack the empirical data to answer such questions, it is still necessary to try to make sense of those findings that have been reported, looking at both trends which are well established and those which challenge the conventional wisdom of how students learn.

Model 1: The Academic Achievement Game (TAAG) Model

Entwistle and Wilson's model (Figure 9.1) is undoubtedly the most picturesque of those so far advanced, and it is also the simplest. It is presented as a game, like Monopoly, in which 'players' define themselves in terms of intellectual and personality attributes and then proceed around a faculty track littered with 'hazard', 'bonus' or 'chance' factors, which simulate aspects of the university environment which may retard or advance their progress. The model summarises three factors which explain academic performance: *predictability* (which is greater in sciences than in arts or social science), based on such summarising factors as good school examination performance; *chance*, in the form of luck in the quality of the course, one's tutor or examinations; and *change*, with students confounding the prediction made from school performance and personality attributes and achieving higher or lower results than expected.

Figure 9.1: The Academic Achievement Game

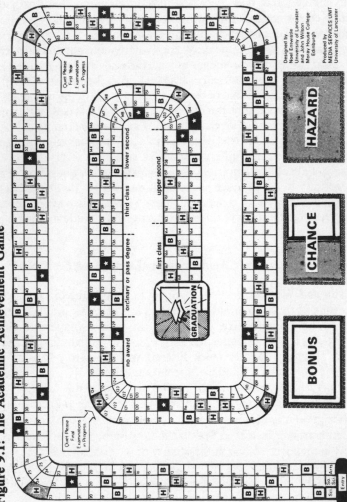

Source: Entwistle and Wilson (1977).

The studies reported in *Degrees of Excellence* were planned and conducted long before most of the research reviewed in this book. The focus of the research was on 'student factors', measured rather crudely, the 'context' being taken into account primarily in terms of the analysis of results by sex and faculty or department of study. In addition to highlighting differences in the predictive variables for performance in arts and science, the Lancaster study suggested that different types of student could be equally successful: besides some who corresponded to the stereotype of the successful student — stable, well motivated, well organised, even ruthless — there were others driven by anxiety and a marked lack of confidence to work long hours who also achieved a high degree of success.

Experience with a wide range of participants suggests that the model represented by TAAG is a useful stimulus to thinking about student processing at university for both staff and students (Wilson, 1978b). It succinctly summarises the research evidence on student performance, and does attempt to simulate some aspects of the interaction between the student and the course of study. Its weakness is the dominant part played in the game by chance factors rather than by conscious choice and determination to succeed; nor does it illustrate the positive influence of teaching and peers on the process of learning and the student's self-image. But this is not surprising as these aspects were not the focus of the research, and so do not feature in the model.

Model 2: Biggs' Presage, Process, Product Model

Biggs (1978) sees 'study processes', which constitute a complex of tactics, strategies and approaches, as mediating between 'presage' factors, such as personal characteristics and institutional variables, and 'product' factors or academic performance. He has advanced a three-factor interactive model in which different combinations of values, motives and strategies produce different 'kinds' of learner, all of whom may be equally successful in higher education.

Biggs' general model is presented in Figure 9.2. The model maintains that the student's approach to his academic work, and the strategies (e.g. rote learning) he adopts in pursuing his studies, are *determined* by such factors as anxiety, induced perhaps by 'fear of failure', or attitudes to university study emanating from expectations and values shaped in the home or school. Study behaviour, in short,

Figure 9.2: General Model of Study Processes

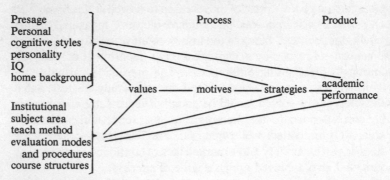

Source: Biggs (1978).

reflects values, assumptions, cognitive style and basic personality structure.

On this view, the research problem is to map out individual characteristics and to relate them to performance. The Study Process Questionnaire (Figure 9.3) has been devised with these objectives in mind. The scales operationalise those personality variables such as convergence-divergence, intolerance of ambiguity, dogmatism and cognitive complexity, academic values and study habits, which the literature has highlighted as being relevant for predicting academic performance. In direct analysis three of the scales show consistent relationships with performance: (3) academic neuroticism (negative relationship), (6) rote learning, and (7) meaningful learning. Study skills (5) appear to contribute directly only a very small amount to prediction, functioning mainly as an interacting variable.

Figure 9.3: Study Process Questionnaire Scales

1. Pragmatism: grade-oriented; student sees university qualifications as a means to some other end.
2. Academic motivation: intrinsically motivated; sees university study as an end in itself.
3. Academic neuroticism: overwhelmed and confused by demands of course work.
4. Internality: uses internal, self-determined standards of truth, not external authority.
5. Study skills: works consistently, reviews regularly, schedules work.
6. Rote learning: centres on facts and details and rote-learns them.
7. Meaningful learning: reads widely and relates material to what is already known: oriented to understand all input material.
8. Test anxiety: worries about tests, exams, fear of failure.
9. Openness: student sees university as a place where values are questioned.
10. Class dependence: needs class structure; rarely questions lecturers or texts.

Source: Biggs (1978).

Biggs obtained consistent results with three student samples in a higher order factor analysis of these scale scores in relation to academic performance, and identified three factors (which explained between 57 and 70 per cent of the total variance) which he labelled Reproducing, Internalising and Organising. Correlation of the 80 scale items with each of these factors produced constellations of values, motives and cognitive strategies which made sense in terms of the interactive model proposed (see Figure 9.4).

Figure 9.4: Three Orthogonal Value-Motive-Strategy Dimensions

	Value	Motive	Strategy
Factor I	pragmatism: instrumental values, university is means to another end.	test anxiety, neuroticism: motive to study is fear of failing.	class dependence; fact-rote. Minimax: goals are those defined in the course, no more: rote learned to a reproductive criterion.
Factor II (internalising)	openness, internality: self-growth or actualisa-tion seen as overall goal, university permits this.	academic motivation: intrinsic, what contri-butes to growth is inter-esting, self-motivated.	meaning: work unsatis-fying unless understood and incorporated with existing knowledge. Class only basis for stimulation.
Factor III (organising)	winning through com-petition: university a game to show excellence.	achievement motivation: need for success, low anxiety.	structuring, organising work, meets deadlines, plays the game.

Source: Biggs (1978).

Biggs describes each of these 'types' as follows:

The 'reproducing' person 'sees the university as an instrument, a means to an end'. His motives for studying are then governed by the fear of not achieving that end, so he defines his goals minimally compatible with success, and uses the simplest strategy of learning, i.e. 'reproducing what he is supposed to do and no more'. The 'internalising' type sees the university as 'the place wherein the self actualisation process can take place: the motive is intrinsic, studying is a process of growing (if it weren't for that individual he would drop out) and hence wide reading, interrelating and meaning-ful learning strategies. Growth only takes place if the material is internalised and related to existing knowledge'. The 'organising' person is driven on by the need for achievement, and 'the value...is competing and winning, whether the goals are self-set or not'. 'Successfully to operate on the basis of the 'killer instinct' requires a very cool, low anxiety, highly organised approach to work.' (Systematic organisation, whatever the particular methods, is one of the most consistent correlates of academic achievement.)

There are striking similarities between these three types and some of the high achieving groups identified by the cluster analyses of Entwistle and Wilson's (1977) Lancaster data. What is impressive here is the way Biggs has parsimoniously summarised the variables. Figure 9.5 outlines two possible 'models' of the study process dimensions: on the first (a) individuals may be located in terms of the three factors; on the second (b) the reproducing-internalising dimension is seen to be one axis, with 'organising' a separate one. Biggs links this latter two-factor theory with Marton's 'depth' and 'surface' approach.

Figure 9.5: Alternative Models of Study Process Dimensions

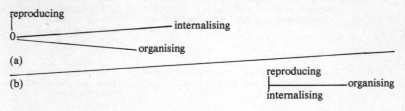

Source: Biggs (1978).

Biggs, then, has identified three different combinations of factors in academic performance: individuals with different values, attitudes, motives and study strategies can still achieve common outcomes. Low level strategies will be effective if they are consistent with the students' general academic philosophy and are not the result of despair or panic. Underachievement may reflect 'mismatch': only if there is congruence between values, motives and strategies will there be effective achievement. A student who believes he is at university for self-realisation and engages in reproductive, rote learning study methods will find himself frustrated and will lose interest in his course: presumably counselling of such a student would aim to promote congruence, perhaps by encouraging the use of appropriate study methods, even if this involved encouraging rote learning among students who only want to do sufficient to scrape a pass in a compulsory subject.

Model 3: Entwistle's Distinctive Approaches Model

At the time of writing (April 1980), final results from the work of Entwistle and his colleagues have not been reported. He has, however, tested several groups of students on the *Lancaster Inventory of Approaches to Learning*, which comprises 15 sub-scales tapping intrinsic, extrinsic and achievement motivation as well as the variables identified by Pask, Marton and Biggs, and related results to academic achievement. A factor analysis of the responses of 767 first year students (Entwistle, Hanley and Hounsell, 1979) identified four factors which explained 56 per cent of the overall variance in the correlational matrix, viz. (1) deep approach/comprehension learning, (2) surface approach/operation learning, (3) organised, achievement-oriented studying, and (4) stable extraversion.

The first three of these factors are reminiscent of Biggs' dimensions, but Entwistle draws attention to stylistic differences in the processes of study. Adoption of a deep approach, for example, is not identical with orientation towards meaning 'as it clearly also involved tendencies towards superficiality, i.e. towards the pathology of globetrotting'. Within the reproducing orientation, also, he suggested one could identify 'both the surface approach with its emphasis on memorisation of facts and definitions, and the concentration on detailed procedures and factual evidence which is the hallmark of operation learning'.

Shortened versions of the scales provided effective predictors in three minor analyses of first year performance; from one of these Entwistle speculated that 'globetrotting' (failure to use supportive evidence) may be more heavily penalised in first year examinations than 'improvidence' (failure to move beyond factual details, or to see wider interconnections).

On the basis of these results, Entwistle advances a tentative model (see Figure 9.6) of student learning which he explains as follows:

The first three columns of the diagram describe the factor structure of the inventory, while the fourth column indicates the overlap that was found between approach and style of learning. The main advance provided by this figure is to isolate four distinct processes of learning, all of which are essential to a deep level of understanding.

Figure 9.6: Categories Describing Distinctive Approaches to Learning

Factor	Orientation and intention	Motivation (personality type)	Approach or style	Process		Outcome
				Stage I	Stage II	
I	Understanding	Intrinsic (Autonomous and syllabus-free)	Deep approach/ versatile	All four processes below used appropraitely to reach understanding		Deep level of understanding
			Comprehension learning	Building overall description of content area	Reorganising incoming information to relate to previous knowledge or experience and establishing personal meaning	Incomplete understanding attributable to globetrotting
II	Reproducing	Extrinsic and fear of failure	Operation learning	Detailed attention to evidence and steps in the argument	Relating evidence to conclusion and maintaining a critical, objective stance	Incomplete understanding attributable to improvidence
		(Anxious and syllabus-bound)	Surface approach	Memorisation	Overlearning	Surface level of understanding
III	Achieving high grades	Hope for success (Stable, self-confident, and ruthless)	Organised/ achievement orientated	Any combination of the six above processes considered appropriate to perceived task requirements and criteria of assessment.		High grades with or without understanding

Source: Entwistle, Hanley and Housnell (1979).

These processes are shown as occurring in two stages. The first stage involves initial attention either to the overall description (comprehension learning) or to the details of the evidence and to steps in the argument (operation learning). This initial focus of attention leads on to the second stage of considering relationships, which may involve either examining links between ideas or concepts and with personal experience (comprehension learning), or the way pieces of evidence fit together to build up a logical argument (operation learning). To reach a deep level of understanding all four processes would normally be required, but our factor analyses suggest a tendency for each factor identified to have a pathology, as well as a desirable attribute. The orientation towards understanding may be accompanied by a tendency towards the superficiality identified with globetrotting. The orientation towards reproducing may be partially compensated by the attention to detail found in operation learning. And finally the orientation towards success may sacrifice understanding for attainment, unless a demand for full understanding is built into the criteria of assessment.

Model 4: Laurillard's Interactionist Model

Both Biggs and Entwistle approach student learning as educational psychologists: their background and training lead them to search for

Figure 9.7: Laurillard's Model of the Processes of Student Learning

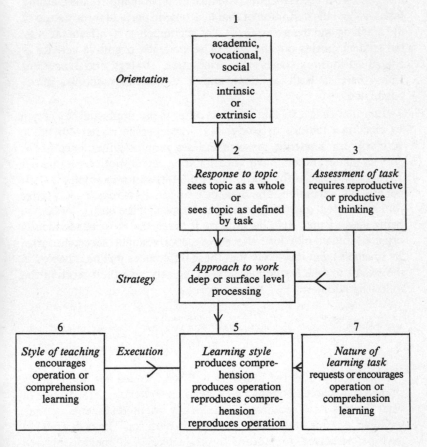

(N.B. Directional lines are 'influences'.)

Source: Laurillard (1978).

consistent traits within individuals which may explain their approach to study, and this explains their emphasis on assessing personality, motivation and attitudes and the interrelationship between these variables and academic performance. Their assumption is that, whatever the differences between learning tasks, individuals will still tend to approach them in a recognisably consistent way.

Laurillard's model by contrast is interactionist and stresses the importance of the student's perception of the context in which learning tasks are located for determining the approach the student will adopt (see Figure 9.7). The model reflects both how individual differences between students influence their perception of the learning task and how the definition of that task, and in particular the nature of the teaching and the assessment that accompanies it, affects the way the student carries out the task, The student's cognitive activity is conceived in three stages, viz. orientation, strategy and execution. Thus there is both a linear and a causal interactionist effect postulated.

Laurillard suggests that students differ in the emphasis they attach to basic orientations to study. (1) Some pursue higher education primarily for academic reasons and are genuinely interested in the subject matter; others have vocational or career motives; a number have social reasons for study, being interested, for example, in their general self-education. The balance between these reasons will differ for each student and the demands and appeal of the particular course being studied may also be important (even the most academically oriented student may lose interest in a poorly taught 'service' course, for example), but it is likely that these differences will be reflected in the extent to which students apply themselves to their work in the following manner:

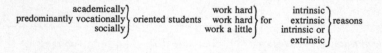

$$\left. \begin{matrix} \text{academically} \\ \text{predominantly vocationally} \\ \text{socially} \end{matrix} \right\} \text{oriented students} \quad \left. \begin{matrix} \text{work hard} \\ \text{work hard} \\ \text{work a little} \end{matrix} \right\} \text{for} \quad \left. \begin{matrix} \text{intrinsic} \\ \text{extrinsic} \\ \text{intrinsic or} \\ \text{extrinsic} \end{matrix} \right\} \text{reasons}$$

Intrinsically oriented students will tend to see the topic being studied as a whole (2): they will seek to understand it, irrespective of what the task itself requires. Extrinsically oriented students will see the topic in terms of the task they have to perform. The task itself (3) may be perceived to require 'reproductive' (i.e. memorising) or 'productive' thinking, involving the ability to go 'beyond the information given'. Perception of the demands of the task influences the strategy the student adopts (4). It is maintained that intrinsically oriented students will take a 'deep' approach, irrespective of the task requirements, while extrinsic students will conform to the demands of the task. Thus the latter will adopt a 'surface' approach if the task requires reproduction, but they are capable of deeper processing if that is demanded. The important point is that extrinsic students respond to the situation rather than defining it. The strategy a student adopts, i.e. the approach he takes to the task, together with the style of teaching and the nature of the specific content being studied, all influence the execution or performance of that task. A student adopting a deep approach will reproduce whatever the teaching encourages (6), but he will also produce what it does not encourage, thus achieving a balanced understanding that includes both operation and comprehension learning. If a student takes a 'surface' approach, however, he will reproduce only that part of the teaching that the learning task requires. Laurillard speculates that the active 'depth' student may be the 'cue-seeker' who, in Perry's terms, takes personal responsibility for his own progress by seeking understanding both by personal application and from tutors when the teaching does not provide adequate explanation or guidance.

Model 5: Wilson's Developmental Model

The models of Biggs, Entwistle and Laurillard present a snapshot of different 'types' of learner interacting with conceptually difficult academic subject matter. Entwistle and Biggs stress that basic personality structure, cognitive style and prior experience of learning will cause students to approach different tasks in recognisably consistent ways, taking account, of course, of the student's perceptions of the demands of assessment. Laurillard sees the student as a decision-maker, capable of choosing his own orientation and strategy of approach and responsive to the context as he perceives it.

None of these models, however, relates types of learner clearly to level of academic performance, nor does any appear to allow for the possibility of the development of the student's capacity to learn, either through maturation or through the influence of higher education. Roy Heath's model (1964), which was discussed in Chapter 4, did show that it is possible to conceive of students both as 'types' and as individuals developing towards greater maturity over their years at college. The model outlined in Figure 9.8 attempts to integrate the

Figure 9.8: A Developmental Model of Student Learning

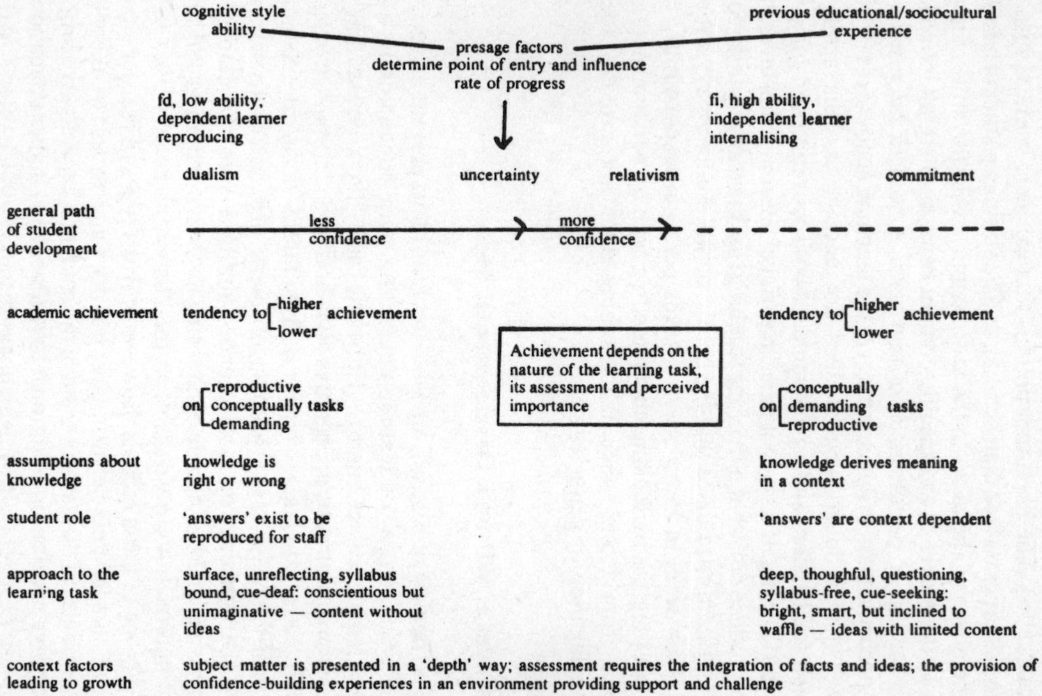

	cognitive style ability	presage factors	previous educational/sociocultural experience
		determine point of entry and influence rate of progress	

		uncertainty	relativism	commitment

general path
of student
development

fd, low ability,
dependent learner
reproducing

fi, high ability,
independent learner
internalising

dualism

←—— less
confidence

more ——→
confidence

academic achievement

tendency to ⌈ higher achievement
⌊ lower

tendency to ⌈ higher achievement
⌊ lower

⌈ reproductive
on ⌊ conceptually tasks
demanding

⌈ conceptually ⌉ tasks
on ⌊ demanding ⌋
reproductive

> Achievement depends on the
> nature of the learning task,
> its assessment and perceived
> importance

assumptions about
knowledge

knowledge is
right or wrong

knowledge derives meaning
in a context

student role

'answers' exist to be
reproduced for staff

'answers' are context dependent

approach to the
learning task

surface, unreflecting, syllabus
bound, cue-deaf: conscientious but
unimaginative — content without
ideas

deep, thoughful, questioning,
syllabus-free, cue-seeking;
bright, smart, but inclined to
waffle — ideas with limited content

context factors
leading to growth

subject matter is presented in a 'depth' way; assessment requires the integration of facts and ideas; the provision of
confidence-building experiences in an environment providing support and challenge

available research findings in a developmental model of student learning.

The model takes account of Perry and Heath's findings that a sizable proportion of students develop new conceptions of what studying in higher education involves over their years in college. The model maintains that the general effect of study is to awaken students' minds by requiring them to think relativistically. Students move from a relatively passive conception of their role as learners at entry (anxious, uncertain, lacking in skills, looking for 'answers', and with no record of success to give them confidence) to role conceptions which are more active, thoughtful, questioning and challenging, and which reflect growth in confidence in themselves as learners. The starting position on the continuum will depend on 'presage' factors; students at elite institutions, such as Harvard, are likely to be more 'advanced' than those at red-brick universities or in diploma-level higher education: the ease and speed of progress along the continuum will reflect presage factors and the nature of the teaching, learning and assessment context. Broadbent (1975) has remarked that 'the lesson of cognitive psychology is that each of us acquires during life certain strategies of encoding the outside world, or organising memory, and of proceeding from one step in an operation to the next, and that these may be highly general in their later use'. It is likely that students with tendencies towards comprehension learning, field independence and divergence will even at entry reflect the more sophisticated, relativistic style of thinking about issues which higher education seeks to develop, and which corresponds to the Robbins Report's aim of promoting the general powers of the mind. Students with tendencies towards operation learning, field dependence and convergence are likely to have the greatest problems acquiring such styles of thinking and will require most help in 'learning how to learn'.

The model conceives of the various approaches to study displayed by students as correlates of dualistic and relativistic thinking. The dualistic conception defines knowing at the lowest level of Bloom's taxonomy: learning is passive, reproductive, surface and verbatim commitment to memory; such a conception implies cue deafness and being syllabus bound. Relativistic conceptions define knowing as comprehending: learning is understanding the wider context in which ideas are located, and this implies a process of relating, questioning and making meaning. Such deep, thoughtful approaches are characteristic of students responsive to and alert for 'cues' and of the syllabus free. Relativistic thinkers implicitly have more control over their thinking process and have more flexible strategies: in Piagetian terms they have substituted more sophisticated conceptions of learning for less sophisticated, but the latter are still available if the context demands them.

Growth along the continuum depends partly on presage factors and partly on how students are processed in higher education. Just as the Selkirk grace expresses a philosophy of man and his belly,[1] so one can define different conditions under which intellectual and moral development will or will not occur. Some students are incapable of growth however well they are taught and counselled; some are capable of development if they are given the 'right' academic treatment; some do change *despite* the academic treatment — the influence of the peer group may in some cases be the most potent factor; some change *because* of the academic context. There are many possibilities in the above for exploring the 'impact' of higher education on the student in terms of Astin's model which was described earlier.

In Chapter 3 the context factors in learning were considered. It is the case that many courses do not demand relativistic thinking for high academic performance, but rather require a great deal of low level memorising of detail. Even courses in literature, philosophy and educational 'ideas' can communicate bodies of knowledge as facts for regurgitation, rather than as ways of thinking in which the excitement of the original formulation is rediscovered. Diligent, organised, systematic students will have no difficulty shining in such courses; but relativistic students, especially if to their independence of mind is added a radical stance, may find it difficult to sustain interest and may resent the need to master detail which 'can be looked up in the textbook'; in extreme cases they may transfer or withdraw. Other courses, especially in first year, may make intellectual demands higher than the typical first year student can cope with and this, as well as factual overloading, especially in the sciences, may be a curriculum-induced factor in student failure.

The model recognises that context factors may lead to growth along the continuum: the role staff play, the structure of teaching and assessment, effective teachback and counselling — all may help the student to grow in confidence as a learner. The learning environment must, as Perry argued, provide both support and challenge. A fuller discussion of these aspects in relation to the learner is reserved for the conclusion.

Students may acquire a considerable body of factual knowledge and skills in higher education without moving from a basically dualistic conception of learning. A proportion may be able to imitate the forms of relativistic thinking in relation to their own subject, but be unable to transfer such forms more widely: graduates on teacher education courses often see issues in black and white terms. In a recent discussion on professionalism, for example, one student asked me why, as head of department, I allowed certain material on the topic to appear in the departmental handout when I was arguing against the conception of professionalism it represented! Students, in short, may receive their degrees and diplomas without developing intellectually at all — simply having become 'well-informed bores' — or without acquiring that flexibility of thinking and method of attack on issues that Robbins saw as a main aim of higher education.

It is important not to be too pessimistic, however. Figure 9.8 is maintaining, admittedly on a thin empirical base, that the normal pattern of student growth is from dualism to relativism, and that this involves a change in the student's conception of what learning involves. In many cases, especially among the ablest honours students, progress goes further as study leads to commitment to the field of study and its values, a commitment which lasts long after higher education is over. The point of entry on the continuum reflects presage factors, and these together with context will affect progress along it. The usefulness of relativistic thinking for academic success will depend on the nature of the learning task, the assessment linked to it and the student's perception of both, as well as his willingness to conform to the regime of the department in which he is studying. Obviously it is institutional factors such as the teaching programme, counselling facilities and the social context, such as the peer group, which are most susceptible to manipulation and which can be used to promote or retard intellectual growth. It is to how such thinking might be promoted that we turn finally.

Note

1. The Selkirk grace, recited at Burns Suppers, states:
       'Some hae meat but canna eat,
       Some wad eat but want it;
       But we hae meat and we can eat,
       Sae let the Lord be thankit.'

10 IMPLICATIONS FOR IMPROVING LEARNING, TEACHING AND ASSESSMENT

The developmental model outlined in the previous chapter implies that many students need to be helped to acquire a sophisticated conception of active, relativistic learning. Equally, however, if we wish to require students to develop critical intellectual attitudes and commitment to study, we must pay attention to the curriculum they are offered. In this final chapter I want to review the usefulness of the help normally offered to students, particularly in the form of study manuals, and to consider the curricular implications of the findings.

Study manuals and individual counselling are the two forms of help normally offered to students seeking advice on how to study. Manuals offer general, prescriptive advice: a manual, according to Webster's Dictionary, is 'a book containing in concise form the principles, rules and directions needed for the mastery of an art, science or skill'. More than a hundred study manuals exist, and there have been a number of developments within the genre recently. Counselling, on the other hand, is individual, problem-oriented and specific, relating general theory to the student's emotional, social and intellectual needs. Study manuals attempt to provide general advice in a personal way. They are certainly useful for bringing to mind a range of factors relevant for studying, and they can have a consciousness-raising effect, like all good textbooks. It is illuminating, for example, to know of 'gumption traps' (Pirsig, 1974) and how to avoid them. But study manuals, like those for cars or motor cycles, rarely help with your particular problem or, alternatively, like the 'Home Doctor', you can recognise all the symptoms of every ailment (including gout) in yourself. It requires considerable self-awareness to recognise the advice that is relevant, and greater strength of mind to apply it. The evidence on their effectiveness is not very impressive: Maddox (1963) admits that 'no one has ever proved experimentally that reading a book on how to study leads to improvement, but those students who have read such books usually say that they found them helpful'. Counselling, on the other hand, does help students directly, and appears to be cost effective (Wankowski, 1979).

Main (1980) provides a useful guide to the content of some of the more prominent study manuals. Manuals may offer prescriptive advice at different levels of specificity, or they may model the skill in question. An example of the latter is the summaries provided in the tape-book presentation by Haynes *et al*. (1977). Useful prescriptive advice may be offered on such matters as equipment (calculators, paper size, etc.) but it is when one gets into more complex areas, such as essay writing and problem solving, that traditional advice often becomes difficult to apply. Gibbs (1977) and Thomas and Harri-Augstein (1978) have attempted to help the student realise that he must become self-critical of the approaches he adopts in the light of others that are potentially available to him.

Gibbs (1977), in association with Northedge, has developed workshops which aim to help the student 'to articulate his own conception of the purposes and processes of his own studying'. A series of exercises has been devised in which note-taking or evaluation of written work is practised. Students first attempt the task individually, then in pairs compare their response, again in fours, and finally as a group. The tutor has a supportive, questioning role: the approach is very successful at getting students thinking and talking about differences in perception of learning tasks. But it is not altogether clear what students learn from this approach, or whether, at the end of the day, it helps them write better essays or take more useful lecture notes.

A similar criticism can be levelled at the ambitious, multi-media package developed at Brunel by Thomas and Harri-Augstein, and entitled 'The Art and Science of Getting a Degree'. Part I of the package is a 'Red Book' which is structured and illustrated in such a way — it looks a proper dog's breakfast! — that it acts as a kind of surrogate tutor, prodding and challenging the student and constantly reminding him by self-questioning and interpolated students' comments that the printed word is fallible and that the reality of the student's own experience is the only valid truth-test. Students who wish to explore ideas about learning further are referred to a 'Blue Book' which comprises a daunting collection of articles and tapes on the theory of learning.

The advice in the Red Book owes much to the ideas of Pirsig (1974) and Pask (1975). It attempts to combine 'an experiential "Zen-like" approach with a rigorous, empirical, scientific one'; it includes awareness-raising exercises, offers support to the learner as he reflects upon how he learns, and gives guidance on how learning competence may be evaluated. Some of these techniques, such as the reading recorder, which has been developed at Brunel, do appear to be helpful to students; the approach to learning which is encouraged through the structuring of topics and ideas into meaningful networks, has also been shown to be effective (Pask, 1977). But how useful is the advice for coping with learning tasks in higher education? One student's reactions sum up some of my misgivings: 'It'll take us months to find out whether all this is worth it! It's hard work, and it's taking up all our spare time!' The Red Book makes a valiant attempt to personalise learning and therefore may have some value at communicating the general idea of an active, relating approach to learning; as Smith (1978) has remarked, arts and social science students belonging to a particular (non-conformist?) student sub-culture would find the style stimulating, but for the average student particularly in science and technology, it might appear too 'way out' to be taken seriously. Despite claims that the tools and procedures can lead to improvements in learning competence of 200 to 300 per cent and more, the empirical evidence is rather thin. Moreover, on a course which demands primarily a rote learning approach, the technique might even widen the gap between the student and successful adaptation.

One of the main lessons from the studies reviewed in this book is the importance of studying what students themselves tell us: the strength of the work of Perry, Marton, Pask and others is that they show us, through extended quotations, *how* students conceive of their role in well-defined contexts, *why* they behave as they do, and what kinds of understanding they display. Marton's recent work (Dahlgren and Marton, 1977) is more explicitly diagnostic, focusing on how students interpret everday ideas which are central to the subject matter. Diagnosis is the basis of effective counselling; it involves, as Main (1980) has pointed out, listening to and exploring the student's problem, understanding and relating to him, and assisting him to focus on available solutions. Many students need help with basic skills, and Shaughnessy's (1977) recent work has shown what a sensitive and sympathetic approach can do for even apparently 'hopeless' cases. There would appear to be great scope for the development of study skills workshops providing the above kinds of help at the individual level.

But staff also need more support than they are currently offered. Pamphlets on teaching methods (e.g. Ross and Cockburn, 1978) and the short general courses on teaching and assessment now offered by most universities are rather like staff equivalents of study manuals: they rarely help with specific problems of course construction or evaluation. A more promising approach is being developed by Brown (1978). Eraut (1972) has suggested that consultancy and workshop models may provide support for school staff involved in innovation, and Black and Dockrell (1980) have shown how 'collaborative research' can help in diagnostic evaluation of learning difficulties in some secondary curricular areas. In Australia, Miller (1977) has described the work of a staff development unit in higher education and promising results have been obtained. But the will to change must be present, and that can only come from awareness by staff of the limitations of present models of teaching and assessing and a commitment to invest greater energies in developing alternative models. It is to curricular implications that we turn finally.

Curricular Implications

What are the implications of this study for the curriculum, and in particular for assessment of students? It should be recalled that students study in a social context, and they tailor their behaviour to meet the assessment demands in the most economic manner compatible with the need to maintain academic progress. This general point is borne out in an interesting study by Mechanic (1978) which came to notice too late to be included in Chapter 3. It traces the experience of a small group of post-graduate American PhD students, preparing for nine two-hour written examinations which served a screening function in relation to admission to the final stage of the PhD course. Mechanic both reminds us of the intense anxiety generated by examinations in a supposedly sophisticated group of successful students, and shows how the students develop 'coping' and 'defence' strategies for handling the stress the situation created. The study was first reported in 1960; it serves a useful function here in bringing together some of the themes touched on in earlier chapters.

Mechanic reminds us of the importance of the peer group for many students: the individual student preparing for an examination is in the dark about whether he is working at the 'right' subject matter, or whether he is really taking from it what he should; his reference point is often other students, and how well they appear to be getting on. If he feels he is not doing as well as they are, he will feel anxious, and this may lead to self-questioning and neurosis. Conversely, getting access to a 'key' book in advance of other students can lead to renewed, if temporary, feelings that one is making progress.

Clearly the importance of the peer group will differ for individuals, but two things are suggested by Mechanic's findings: students who do not participate in the 'process of social comparison' are less informed about the exams, feel less competitive and less anxious, but also are less motivated and in general do less well; the second point is that as the examination week approaches, even isolates tend to seek support and discussion of the situation with other students in the same predicament.

Of particular importance in Mechanic's study are the strategies students employ to cope with, and defend, their personality in the face of continuous stress. Students cope through the way they approach preparation: the way they allocate time, decide what to study and choose to go about it. All are anxious, but some are better able to control anxiety than others and to maintain their study plans. Presumably these are the 'organised' successful students of the research literature, but they may also be more realistic in setting out a programme they can keep to.

Students try to control their anxiety by talking with staff and seeking reassurance, by telling themselves that they will pass, by comparing themselves with others in previous years who have passed, by developing in-jokes within the peer group, by seeking comforting clues such as self-tests which show that they 'know' what they have been studying. Some, however, become hostile to staff for imposing a burden they perceive to be unrealistic.

The stress these students experience stems from an examination system which, in the eyes of the staff, is intended to present an intellectual challenge and to encourage intensive, meaningful study. The students do not perceive it that way and resort to academic gamesmanship worthy of Mr Metzger. They lose sight of the purpose of learning and the meaning of issues, and resort to such tricks as learning up quotations, lists of experiments and prestigious names to drop at random into answers with the intention of creating a favourable impression on the staff. There is no reason to doubt that students in Britain employ similar strategies.

Despite wide-ranging debate, traditional essay-type examinations continue to hold sway, particularly in arts and social science, while multiple choice has a significant foothold in science. There is, today, a greater willingness to experiment (cf. Becher *et al.* (1975) and the emergence of such publications as *Assessment in Higher Education* and *Evaluation Newsletter*), but many staff take comfort, perhaps in the student evidence (Siann and Pilliner, 1974; Main, 1980) that examinations are a necessary incentive to work. My major concern, however, is with the *way* students work and the kinds of learning that occur. A variety of modes of assessment is required if all the objectives of a course are to be effectively monitored (Rowntree, 1977). As Mechanic (1978) observes: 'From a faculty [i.e. staff] perspective the goal is. . .to devise learning situations in which the adaptive process is consistent with the values of the profession and the achievement of competence.' This implies academics acquiring a more sophisticated grasp of the relationship between assessment and learning.

A similar point may be made in relation to teaching method. Freire (1970) has remarked that development in personal and social awareness is essential in any educational process which aims to give people intelligent and effective control over their physical and social environment. This is more difficult to achieve within the traditional framework of prescriptive teaching, since it renders learners dependent upon the activity of the teacher. Indeed, some of the evidence on staff attitudes reviewed in Chapter 3 suggests that they perceive students on a 'deficit' model (Barnes, 1976) much as do teachers working with linguistically disadvantaged children. Formal teaching methods have the effect of reducing students to a role of 'receivers of messages'; they mask the interaction effects of teacher, teaching method and student, which together explain the level of achievement reached. But this is not to say we must abandon lectures: Bligh (1971) has shown that they are effective for conveying information, and lectures have a function in motivating students and modelling 'deep' thinking. But considerable skill, experience and commitment are required and other methods are needed as back-up. Davie (1961) showed how the nineteenth-century Scottish university professor required his students to follow up his delivery by engaging in class debates on the principles raised and to submit to oral examining. Blis and Ogborn (1977) and Roy Heath (1964) emphasise the maturing influence exerted by essays, projects and dissertations: one might go further and state that such exercises provide a needed challenge to the student's intellect and shape his conception of his role as a learner; they teach him to search, explore and think through ideas, and in the process he becomes committed to the pursuit of a topic. Discussion of the completed exercise, as Perry pointed out, can illuminate how the student has conceived of his role as a learner; effective teachback can provide not simply knowledge and understanding, but increased motivation, raised morale and, most important of all, a feeling of trust in the teacher as someone who cares. In short, relativistic frameworks can be both 'caught' from modelling by the teacher and 'taught' through first-hand experience.

Since half of all academic failure occurs in first year, particular attention to the planning of courses at that stage is required; early experiences lay down subsequent patterns of learning, while success or failure may have important implications for motivation. Yet in most courses the first year curriculum is designed to provide a superficial coverage of landmarks in a field of knowledge, usually based on a substantial lecture input. The student is cast in a passive role, isolated and with few friends, surviving in an anxious, uncommitted and even anti-academic peer group. The situation encourages surface processing.

A Copernican revolution of the whole curriculum may be too radical to contemplate, for many would argue that a wide sweep is of value in a foundation course, but there is surely a case for a compromise in which a limited range of important specific competences are taught in formal classes while a significant proportion of the contact time is devoted to closely supervised divergent, creative and active learning which requires the student to go 'beyond the information given'.

Research has a consciousness-raising function: the studies reviewed earlier provide a vocabulary and ways of thinking about students which can assist in guiding the individual and in directing the development of the group. There is always a danger, of course, that the insights gained may blind us to other equally important differences between students than capacity to structure and imaginative independence which have been highlighted here. The conclusion of the present review is that the curriculum and its assessment are the key factors affecting the quality of student learning.

SUGGESTED FURTHER READING

Becker, H.S., Geer, B. and Hughes, E.C. *Making the Grade* (Wiley, New York, 1968). Together with Becker's earlier study *Boys in White* (1961) this provides one of the most illuminating accounts of how American students conceive of and approach the academic demands of the institution.

Bruner, J.S. *The Process of Education* (Random House, New York, 1960). A lucid, succinct review of principles implicit in meaningful learning.

Collier, G., Wilson J. and Tomlinson, P. (eds.) *Values and Moral Development in Higher Education* (Croom Helm, London, 1974). Wide-ranging collection of essays which review philosophical and psychological evidence on moral development, discuss the effects of study in different fields on such development, and examine the effects of context (e.g. residence) on student development.

Entwistle, N.J. *Styles of Learning and Teaching: an Integrative Outline of Educational Psychology* (John Wiley, London, 1981 in press)

—— and Hounsell, D.J. (eds.) *How Students Learn* (Institute for Research and Development in Post Compulsory Education, University of Lancaster, 1975). A good starting point for a study of the psychological literature on learning, introducing the ideas of Pask, Marton and Perry.

——and Wilson, J.D. *Degrees of Excellence: the Academic Achievement Game* (Hodder and Stoughton Educational, London, 1977). Useful for its literature review, its methodology and the evidence on 'types' of students in different subject areas who encounter differing levels of success.

Feldman, K.A. and Newcomb, T.M. *The Impact of College on Students*, 2 vols. (Jossey-Bass, San Francisco, 1969). Summarises and reviews an impressive range of (mostly American) studies. As useful for demonstrating pitfalls to avoid as for the results actually obtained.

Hills, P.J. (ed.) *Study Courses and Counselling* (Research into Higher Education Monographs, Society for Research into Higher Education, Guildford, 1979). Essays reviewing British developments in the promotion of 'learning to learn' among students.

Hunt, D.E. and Sullivan, E.V. *Between Psychology and Education* (Dryden Press, Illinois, 1974). An attempt to reconcile a developmental perspective and the idea of fixed traits, and to consider the most appropriate educational 'treatments' to promote growth.

Main, A. *Encouraging Effective Learning* (Scottish Academic Press, Edinburgh, 1980). Basically an account of the author's work with students at the University of Strathclyde: a succinct chapter which summarises theoretical literature, but the counselling and support techniques developed for students are of special interest.

Messick, S. and Associates, *Individuality in Learning* (Jossey-Bass, San Francisco, 1976). Essays on the origins of cognitive styles and their importance for teaching and learning in higher education.

Miller, C.M.L. and Parlett, M. *Up to the Mark* (Society for Research into Higher Education, London, 1974). Illuminating evidence on how staff and students perceive assessment in different departmental contexts at a Scottish university.

Mechanic, D. *Students under Stress: A Study in the Social Psychology of Adaptation* (University of Wisconsin Press, Madison, 1978). A fascinating account of the process whereby postgraduate students prepare for a critical examination: a participant-observer study which illuminates and disturbs.

Parker, C.A. (ed.) *Encouraging Development in College Students* (University of Minnesota Press, Minneapolis, 1978). Essays describing attempts to promote student development along the lines sketched out by Perry, while the Heaths (Douglas and Roy), David Hunt and others provide critical commentary.

Perry, W. *Forms of Intellectual and Ethical Development in the College Years: A Scheme* (Holt, Rinehart and Winston, New York, 1970). A classic: shrewd and penetrating insights into the student condition.

Piaget, J. *Science of Education and the Psychology of the Child* (Longman, London, 1971). Piaget at his most readable: his general theory of learning is as relevant for higher education as for schools.

Pirsig, R.M. *Zen and the Art of Motor Cycle Maintenance: an Inquiry into Values* (Bodley Head, London, 1974). Well worth reading: a profound and perceptive book which introduces some of the key issues about learning in concrete, specific contexts.

Rowntree, D. *Assessing Students: How Shall we Know Them?* (Harper and Row, London, 1977). A sensitive discussion of the relationship between assessment and learning which helps to clarify both purposes and techniques.

Shaughnessy, M.P. *Errors and Expectations* (Oxford University Press, New York, 1977). Useful to the student counsellor for teaching attitudes and remedial approaches that succeed.

Snyder, B.R. *The Hidden Curriculum* (Massachusetts Institute of Technology Press, Knopf, New York, 1971). An analysis of the pressures on students in a competitive, elite institution.

Tinto, V. 'Dropout from Higher Education: A Theoretical Synthesis of Recent Research', *Review of Educational Research*, vol. 45 (1975), pp. 89-125. A useful 'state of the art' paper on more general issues in success and failure in American higher education.

BIBLIOGRAPHY

Adderley, K.A. and co-authors, *Project Methods in Higher Education* (Society for Research into Higher Education, Guildford, 1975).

Allbrow, M.C. 'The Influence of Accommodation Upon 64 Reading University Students', *British Journal of Sociology*, vol. 17 (1966).

Allport, G.W. *The Functional Autonomy of Motives* (Bobbs Merrill, Indianapolis, 1937).

Asch, S.E. 'Opinions and Social Pressure', *Scientific American*, no. 450 (1955).

Astin, A.W. 'Measurement and Determinants of the Outputs of Higher Education', in Solomon, L.C. and Taubman, P.J. (eds.) *Does College Matter?* (Academic Press, New York, 1973).

—— 'Undergraduate Achievement and Institutional "Excellence"' in Feldman, K.A. (ed.) *College and Student* (Pergamon, New York, 1972).

—— 'The Methodology of Research on College Impact', in Marjoribanks, E. (ed.) *Environments for Learning* (National Foundation for Educational Research, Slough, 1974).

—— *The American Freshman: National Norms for Fall 1978* (Laboratory for Research on Higher Education, University of California, Los Angeles, 1979).

Barnes, D. *From Communication to Curriculum* (Penguin Books, London, 1976).

Beach, L.R. 'Sociability and Academic Achievement in Various Types of Learning Situations', *Journal of Educational Psychology*, vol. 51 (1960), pp. 208-12.

Beard, R.M., Levy, P.M. and Maddox, H. 'Academic Performance at University', *Educational Review*, vol. 16 (1962), pp. 163-74.

——, Bligh, D.A. and Harding, A.G. *Research into Teaching Methods in Higher Education*, 4th edn (Society for Research into Higher Education, Guildford, 1978).

Becher, R.A. and co-authors, *The Drift of Change* (Nuffield Foundation, London, 1975).

Becker, H.S., Geer, B., Hughes, E.C. and Strauss, A.L. *Boys in White* (University of Chicago Press, Chicago, 1961).

—— —— —— *Making the Grade* (Wiley, New York, 1968).

Bernstein, B. 'On the Classification and Framing of Educational Knowledge', in Young, M.F.D. (ed.) *Knowledge and Control* (Collier Macmillan, London, 1971).

Biggs, J.B. 'Study Behaviour and Performance in Objective and Essay Formats', *Australian Journal of Education*, vol. 17 (1973), pp. 157-67.

—— 'Individual and Group Differences in Study Processes', *British Journal of Educational Psychology*, vol. 48 (1978), pp. 266-79.

Black, H.D. and Dockrell, W.B. *Diagnostic Assessment in Geography* (Scottish Council for Research in Education, Edinburgh, 1980).

Bligh, D. *What's the Use of Lectures?* (Penguin, London, 1971).

Blis, J. and Ogborn, J. *Students' Reactions to Undergraduate Science* (Heinemann, London, 1977).

Bloom, B.S. (ed.) *Taxonomy of Educational Objectives: the Classification of Educational Goals, Handbook I: Cognitive Domain* (Longmans, London, 1956).

—— *Human Characteristics and School Learning* (McGraw Hill, New York, 1976).

Bolton, C.D. and Kammeyer, K.W. 'Campus Cultures, Role Orientations and Social Types', in Feldman, K.A. (ed.) *College and Student* (Pergamon, New York, 1972).

Broadbent, D.E. 'Cognitive Psychology and Education', *British Journal of Educational Psychology*, vol. 45 (1975), pp. 162-76.

Brown, G. *Lecturing and Explaining* (Methuen, London, 1978).

—— and Desforges, C. 'Piagetian Psychology and Education: Time for Revision', *British Journal of Educational Psychology*, vol. 47 (1977), pp. 7-17.

—— ——'The Educational Utility of Piaget: A Reply to Shayer', *British Journal of Educational Psychology*, vol. 49 (1979), pp. 277-81.

Bruner, J.S. *The Process of Education* (Random House, New York, 1960).

—— *Toward a Theory of Instruction* (Norton, New York, 1966).

——, Goodnow, J.J. and Austin, G.A. *A Study of Thinking* (Wiley, New York, 1956).

——, Olver, R.R. and Greenfield, P.M. *Studies in Cognitive Growth* (Wiley, New York, 1966).

Burchill, J. 'Biology Across the Interface', *Scottish Association for Biological Education Newsletter*, no. 1 (1978).

Chibnall, B. ' The Sussex Experience', in Hills, P.J. (ed.) *Study Courses and Counselling* (Research into Higher Education Monographs, Society for Research into Higher Education, Guildford,

1979).

Chickering, A.W. *Education and Identity* (Jossey-Bass, San Francisco, 1969).

Clark, B.R. and Trow, M. 'The Organisational Context', in Newcomb, T.M. and Wilson, E.K. (eds.) *College Peer Groups* (Aldine, Chicago, 1966).

Coleman, J.S. *The Adolescent Society* (Free Press, New York, 1961).

Collier, G., Wilson, J. and Tomlinson, P. (eds.) *Values and Moral Development in Higher Education* (Croom Helm, London, 1974).

Coombs, P.H. *The World Educational Crisis: A Systems Analysis* (Oxford University Press, London, 1971).

Cronbach, L.J. 'How Can Instruction be Adapted to Individual Differences?' in Gagné, R. (ed.) *Learning and Individual Differences* (Merrill, Columbus, 1967).

Dahlgren, L.O. and Marton, F. 'Investigations into the Learning and Teaching of Basic Concepts in Economics', in Bonboir, A. (ed.) *Instructional Design in Higher Education: Innovations in Curricula and Teaching* (European Association for Research and Development in Higher Education, Louvain la Neuve, 1977).

Daniel, J.S. 'Learning Styles and Strategies: The Work of Gordon Pask', in Entwistle, N.J. and Hounsell, D.J. (eds.) *How Students Learn* (Institute for Research and Development in Post Compulsory Education, University of Lancaster, 1975).

Davie, G. *The Democratic Intellect: Scotland and Her Universities in the 19th Century* (Edinburgh University Press, Edinburgh, 1961).

Dewey, J. *Democracy and Education* (Macmillan, New York, 1917).

Donaldson, M. *Children's Minds* (Fontana, Collins, Glasgow, 1978).

Dressel, P.L. *Handbook of Academic Evaluation* (Jossey-Bass, San Francisco, 1976).

Eddy, E.R. *The College Influence on Student Character* (American Council on Education, Washington, 1959).

Elkind, D. *Children and Adolescents* (Oxford University Press, New York, 1970).

Ellison, A. and Simon, B. 'Does College Make a Person Healthy and Wise?' in Solomon, L.C. and Taubman, P.J. (eds.) *Does College Matter?* (Academic Press, New York, 1973).

Elton, L.R.B. and Laurillard, D.M. 'Trends in Research on Student

Learning', *Studies in Higher Education*, vol. 4 (1979), pp. 87-102.

Entwistle, N.J. 'How Students Learn: Information Processing, Intellectual Development and Confrontation', *Higher Education Bulletin* (Institute for Post Compulsory Education, University of Lancaster), vol. 3 (1975), pp. 129-48.

—— 'Strategies of Learning and Studying: Recent Research Findings', *British Journal of Educational Studies*, vol. 25 (1977), pp. 225-38.

—— 'Knowledge Structures and Styles of Learning: A Summary of Pask's Recent Research', *British Journal of Educational Psychology*, vol. 48 (1978), pp. 255-65.

—— 'Stages, Levels, Styles or Strategies: Dilemmas in the Description of Thinking', *Educational Review*, vol. 31 (1979), pp. 123-32.

——, Percy, K.A. and Nisbet, J.B. *Educational Objectives and Academic Performance in Higher Education*, 2 vols. (Mimeographed Report, Department of Educational Research, University of Lancaster, 1971).

—— and Percy, K.A. 'Critical Thinking or Conformity? An Investigation of the Aims and Outcomes of Higher Education', *Research into Higher Education, 1973* (Society for Research into Higher Education, London, 1974).

—— and Hounsell, D.J. (eds.) *How Students Learn* (Institute for Research and Development in Post Compulsory Education, University of Lancaster, 1975).

—— and Wilson, J.D. *Degrees of Excellence: the Academic Achievement Game* (Hodder and Stoughton Educational, London, 1977).

—— and Hanley, M. 'Personality, Cognitive Style and Students' Learning Strategies', *Higher Education Bulletin* (Institute for Post Compulsory Education, University of Lancaster), vol. 6 (1977), pp. 23-44.

—— —— and Ramsden, P. 'How Students Learn and Study' (*Second Progress Report to Social Science Research Council*, September 1978).

—— —— and Ratcliffe, G. 'Approaches to Learning and Levels of Understanding', *British Journal of Educational Research*, vol. 5 (1979), pp. 99-114.

—— —— and Hounsell, D. 'Identifying Distinctive Approaches to Studying', *Higher Education*, vol. 8 (1979), pp. 365-80.

Eraut, M. *In Service Education for Innovation* (National Council for Educational Technology, Occasional Paper 4, London, 1972).

Etzioni, A. *A Comparative Analysis of Complex Organisations* (Free Press, Glencoe, Illinois, 1961).

Feldman, K.A. and Newcomb, T.M. *The Impact of College on Students*, 2 vols. (Jossey-Bass, San Francisco, 1969).

Fontana, D. *Personality and Education* (Open Books, London, 1977).

Fransson, A. 'On Qualitative Differences in Learning: IV — Effects of Intrinsic Motivation and Extrinsic Test Anxiety on Process and Outcome', *British Journal of Educational Psychology*, vol. 47 (1977), pp. 244-57.

Freire, P. *Pedagogy of the Oppressed* (Penguin, Harmondsworth, 1972).

Fromm, E. *The Fear of Freedom* (Routledge and Kegan Paul, London, 1942).

—— *The Sane Society* (Holt, Rinehart and Winston, New York, 1955).

—— *The Anatomy of Human Destructiveness* (Jonathan Cape, London, 1974).

Gaff, J.G., Crombag, H.F.M. and Chang, T.M. 'Environments for Learning in a Dutch University', *Higher Education*, vol. 5 (1976), pp. 285-99.

Gage, N.L. (ed.) *The Psychology of Teaching Methods* (University of Chicago Press, Chicago, 1976).

Gagné, R.M. *The Conditions of Learning* (Holt, Rinehart and Winston, New York, 1965).

—— 'The Learning Basis of Teaching Methods', in Gage, N.L. (ed.) *The Psychology of Teaching Methods* (University of Chicago Press, Chicago, 1976).

Gamson, Z.F. 'Utilitarian and Normative Orientations Toward Education', *Sociology of Education*, vol. 39 (1966), pp. 46-73.

—— 'Performance and Personalism in Student-Faculty Relations', in Feldman, K.A. (ed.) *College and Student* (Pergamon, New York, 1972).

Gardner, R.W., Holzman, P.S., Klein, G.S., Linton, H.B. and Spence, D.P. 'Cognitive Control: A Study of Individual Consistencies in Cognitive Behaviour', *Psychological Issues*, monograph 4 (1959).

Gibbs, G.I. *Learning to Study: A Guide to Running Group Sessions* (Institute of Educational Technology, The Open University, Milton Keynes, 1977).

Goldschmid, B. and Goldschmid, M.L. 'Peer Teaching in Higher

Education: A Review', *Higher Education*, vol. 5 (1976), pp. 9-33.

Goldschmid, M.L. 'Teaching and Learning in Higher Education: Recent Trends', *Higher Education*, vol. 5 (1976), pp. 437-56.

Haan, N., Smith, M.R. and Block, J. 'The Moral Reasoning of Young Adults', *Journal of Personality and Social Psychology* vol. 10 (1968), pp. 183-201.

Hakstian, A.R. 'The Effects of Type of Examination Anticipated on Test Preparation and Performance', *Journal of Educational Research*, vol. 64 (1971), pp. 319-24.

Harvey, O.J., Hunt, D.E. and Schroder, H.M. *Conceptual Systems and Personality Organisation* (Wiley, New York, 1961).

Hatch, S. *Student Residence* (Society for Research into Higher Education, Monograph no. 4, London, 1968).

Haynes, L.J., Hills, P.J., Groves, P.D. and Moyes, R.B. *Effective Learning: A Practical Guide for Students* (Tetradon Publications, Shalford, Surrey, 1977).

Heath, D.H. *Explorations of Maturity* (Appleton Century Crofts, New York, 1965).

—— 'A Model of Becoming a Liberally Educated and Mature Student', in Parker, C.A. (ed.) *Encouraging Development in College Students* (University of Minnesota, Minneapolis, 1978).

Heath, D.H. *The Reasonable Adventurer* (University of Pittsburgh Press, Pittsburgh, 1964).

—— 'Personality and Development of Students in Higher Education', in Parker, C.A. (ed.) *Encouraging Development in College Students* (University of Minnesota Press, Minneapolis, 1978).

Hills, P.J. *The Self Teaching Process* (Croom Helm, London, 1976).

—— (ed.) *Study Courses and Counselling* (Research into Higher Education Monographs, Society for Research into Higher Education, Guildford, 1979).

Hollingdale, R.J. (ed.) Nietzsche, F. *Twilight of the Idols* and *The Anti Christ* (Penguin, Harmondsworth, 1968).

Holloway, C. *Learning and Problem Solving: Part 1, Block 4 of Cognitive Psychology* (Open University Press, Milton Keynes, 1978).

Holzman, P.S. and Gardner, R.W. 'Levelling-Sharpening and Memory Organisation', in Sperry, L. (ed.) *Learning Performance and Individual Differences* (Scott Foresman, Illinois, 1972).

Hounsell, D. and Ramsden, P. 'Roads to Learning', in *Course Design and Student Learning* (Society for Research into Higher Education Annual Conference, Guildford, 1977).

Hudson, L. *Contrary Imaginations* (Methuen, London, 1966).

—— *Frames of Mind* (Methuen, London, 1968).

Hunt, D.E. 'Theorists are Persons, Too: On Preaching What you Practice', in Parker, C.A. (ed.) *Encouraging Development in College Students* (University of Minnesota, Minneapolis, 1978).

—— and Sullivan, E.V. *Between Psychology and Education* (Dryden Press, Illinois, 1974).

Huntley, C.W. 'Changes in Values During the Four Years of College', in Feldman, K.A. (ed.) *College and Student* (Pergamon, New York, 1972).

Hurd, D.P. *New Directions in Teaching Secondary School Science* (Rand McNally, Chicago, 1970).

Joyce, B.R. and Weil, M. *Models of Teaching* (Prentice Hall, Englewood Cliffs, 1972).

Kagan, J. 'Reflection-Impulsivity: the Generality and Dynamics of Conceptual Tempo', *Journal of Abnormal Psychology*, vol. 71 (1966), pp. 17-24.

Kelly, G.A. *The Psychology of Personal Constructs* (Norton, New York, 1955).

Knefelkamp, L.L. and Slepitza, R. 'A Cognitive Developmental Model of Career Development: An Adaptation of the Perry Scheme', in Parker, C.A. (ed.) *Encouraging Development in College Students* (University of Minnesota, Minneapolis, 1978).

Kogan, N. 'Sex Differences in Creativity and Cognitive Styles', in Messick, S. (ed.) *Individuality in Learning* (Jossey-Bass, San Francisco, 1976).

Kohlberg, L. 'Development of Moral Character and Ideology', in Hoffman, M.L. and Hoffman, L.W. (eds.) *Review of Child Development Research* (Russell Sage Foundation, New York, 1964).

—— 'Moral Education in the Schools: a Developmental View', *School Review* (1966), pp. 1-30.

—— and Kramer, R. 'Continuities and Discontinuities in Childhood and Adult Moral Development', *Human Development*, vol. 12 (1969), pp. 93-120.

Kuhn, T.S. *The Structure of Scientific Revolutions* (University of Chicago Press, Chicago, 1962).

Laurillard, D. 'A Study of the Relationship between some of the Cognitive and Contextual Factors in Student Learning' (unpublished PhD thesis, University of Surrey, 1978).

Lewis, B.N. 'Avoidance of Aptitude–Treatment Trivialities', in Messick, S. (ed.) *Individuality in Learning* (Jossey-Bass, San

Francisco, 1976).

Lindsay, P.H. and Norman, D.A. *Human Information Processing* (Academic Press, New York, 1972).

Lipset, S.M. and Lowenthal, L. (eds.) *Culture and Social Character* (Free Press, New York, 1961).

Lucas, C.J. 'Changing Concepts in Student Health', in *Students in Need* (Society for Research into Higher Education, Guildford, 1978).

McKellar, P. *Imagination and Thinking* (Cohen and West, London, 1957).

MacKenzie, N., Grant, M. and Jones, A.C. *Teaching and Learning: An Introduction to New Methods and Resources in Higher Education* (UNESCO, Paris, 1970).

McLeish, J. 'Systems, Models, Simulations and Games in Education: a Description and Bibliography', in Armstrong, R.H.R. and Taylor, J.L. (eds.) *Instructional Simulation Systems in Higher Education* (Cambridge Monographs on Teaching Methods no. 2, Cambridge Institute of Education, 1970).

—— 'The Lecture Method', in Gage, N.L. (ed.) *The Psychology of Teaching Methods* (University of Chicago Press, Chicago, 1976).

Maddox H. *How to Study* (Pan Books, London, 1963).

Main, A. *Encouraging Effective Learning* (Scottish Academic Press, Edinburgh, 1980).

Malleson, N. 'The Influence of Emotional Factors on Achievement in University Education', *Sociological Review Monograph*, no. 7 (1963).

Marton, F. 'What Does it Take to Learn?' in Entwistle, N.J. and Hounsell, D.J. (eds.) *How Students Learn* (Institute for Research and Development in Post Compulsory Education, University of Lancaster, 1975).

—— and Säljö, R. 'On Qualitative Differences in Learning: I Outcome and Process', *British Journal of Educational Psychology*, vol. 46 (1976a), pp. 4-11.

—— and Säljö, R. 'On Qualitative Differences in Learning: II Outcome as a Function of the Learner's Conception of the Task', *British Journal of Educational Psychology*, vol. 46 (1976b), pp. 115-27.

Mechanic, D. *Students Under Stress: A Study in the Social Psychology of Adaptation* (University of Wisconsin Press, Madison, 1978).

Messick, S. (ed.) *Individuality in Learning* (Jossey-Bass, San

Francisco, 1976).

Miller, A.H. 'The Role of a Higher Education Unit in Course Design', Paper presented at SERA Conference, St Andrews, 1977 (Office for Research in Academic Methods, Australian National University, Canberra).

Miller, C.M.L. and Parlett, M. *Up to the Mark* (Society for Research into Higher Education, London, 1974).

Morris, P. 'Practical Strategies for Human Learning and Remembering', in Howe, M.J.A. (ed.) *Adult Learning* (Wiley, New York, 1977).

Musgrove, F. *Youth and the Social Order* (Routledge and Kegan Paul, London, 1964).

Muuss, R.E. *Theories of Adolescence* (Random House, New York, 1968).

Newcomb, T.M. *Personality and Social Change: Attitude Formation in a Student Community* (Dryden, New York, 1943).

—— and Wilson, E.K. (eds.) *College Peer Groups* (Aldine, Chicago, (1966).

Open University Course E281: Cashdan, and Lee, V. *Learning Styles: Units 1 and 2* (Open University Press, Milton Keynes, 1971).

Pantages, T.J. and Creedon, C.F. 'Studies of College Attrition: 1950-1975', *Review of Educational Research*, vol. 48 (1978), pp. 49-101.

Parker, C.A. *Encouraging Development in College Students* (University of Minnesota, Minneapolis, 1978).

Parlett, M.L. 'The Syllabus-Bound Student', in Hudson, L. (ed.) *The Ecology of Human Intelligence* (Penguin, Harmondsworth, 1970).

—— and King, J.G. *Concentrated Study* (Society for Research into Higher Education, Monograph 14, London, 1971).

—— in Jamieson, M., Parlett, M.L. and Pocklington, K. *Towards Integration: A Study of Blind and Sighted Children in Ordinary Schools* (National Foundation for Educational Research, Windsor, 1977).

Parnell, R.W. 'Morbidity and Prolonged Illness Among Oxford Undergraduates', *The Lancet*, vol. 1 (1951), pp. 731-3.

Pask, G. *Conversation, Cognition and Learning* (Elsevier, Amsterdam, 1975).

—— 'Conversational Techniques in the Study and Practice of Education', *British Journal of Educational Psychology*, vol. 46 (1976a), pp. 12-25.

—— 'Styles and Strategies of Learning', *British Journal of Educational Psychology*, vol. 46 (1976b), pp. 128-48.
—— *et al. Third Progress Report on S.S.R.C. Research Programme* HR 2708 (System Research Ltd, Richmond, Surrey, 1977).
Payne, J. 'The Place of Psychiatry and Counselling in Higher Education', in *Students in Need* (Society for Research into Higher Education, Guildford, 1978).
Peck, R.F. with Havighurst, R.J. *The Psychology of Character Development* (Wiley, New York, 1960).
Percy, K.A. and Salter, F.W. 'Student and Staff Perceptions and the "Pursuit of Excellence" in British Higher Education', *Higher Education*, vol. 5 (1976), pp. 457-73.
—— and Ramsden, P. *Independent Study: Two Examples from English Higher Education* (Society for Research into Higher Education, Guildford, 1980).
Perry, W. *Forms of Intellectual and Ethical Development in the College Years: A Scheme* (Holt, Rinehart and Winston, New York, 1970).
—— 'Studying and the Student', *Higher Education Bulletin* (Institute for Post Compulsory Education, University of Lancaster), vol. 5 (1977), pp. 119-58.
Peters, R.S. *Ethics and Education* (Allen and Unwin, London, 1966).
Peterson, R.E. *Technical Manual: College Student Questionnaires* (Educational Testing Service, Princeton, 1965a).
—— *On a Typology of College Students* (Research Bulletin, RB 65-9, Educational Testing Service, Princeton, 1965b).
Piaget, J. *Science of Education and the Psychology of the Child* (Longman, London, 1971).
Pirsig, R.M. *Zen and the Art of Motor Cycle Maintenance: an Inquiry into Values* (Bodley Head, London, 1974).
Plumb, J.H. *Crisis in the Humanities* (Penguin, Harmondsworth, 1964).
Polanyi, M. *Personal Knowledge* (Routledge and Kegan Paul, London, 1958).
Ramsden, P. 'Student Learning and Perceptions of the Academic Environment', *Higher Education*, vol. 8 (1979), pp. 411-27.
Robertson, I.T. 'Relationships between Learning Strategy, Attention Deployment and Personality', *British Journal of Educational Psychology*, vol. 48 (1978), pp. 86-91.
Ross, A. and Cockburn, B. *Lecturecraft* (University of Lancaster

School of Education, Teaching in Higher Education Series 1, Lancaster, 1978).

Rowntree, D. *Assessing Students: How Shall We Know Them?* (Harper and Row, London, 1977).

Rudduck, J. *Learning Through Small Group Discussion* (Research into Higher Education Monographs, Society for Research into Higher Education, Guildford, 1978).

Rutter, M., Maughan, B., Mortimore, P. and Ouston, J. *Fifteen Thousand Hours* (Open Books, London 1979).

Sarafino, E.P. and Dimattia, P.A. 'Does Grading Undermine Intrinsic Interest in a College Course?' *Journal of Educational Psychology*, vol. 70 (1978), pp. 916-21.

Schutz, A. 'The Stranger: An Essay in Social Psychology', in *School and Society: A Sociological Reader* (Routledge and Kegan Paul, London, 1971).

Scott, W.A. *Values and Organisations* (Rand McNally, New York, 1965).

Shaughnessy, M.P. *Errors and Expectations* (Oxford University Press, New York, 1977).

Shayer, M. 'Has Piaget's Construct of Formal Operational Thinking any Utility?' *British Journal of Educational Psychology*, vol. 49 (1979), pp. 265-76.

Shipman, M. *Participation and Staff Student Relations in a College of Education* (Society for Research into Higher Education Monograph, London, 1969).

Siann, G. and Pilliner, A. *Students' Questionnaire on Assessment* (Godfrey Thomson Unit for Academic Assessment, University of Edinburgh, 1974).

Small, J.J. *Achievement and Adjustment in the First Year at University* (New Zealand Council for Educational Research, Wellington, 1966).

Smith, M.P. 'Teaching to Learn?', *Studies in Higher Education*, vol. 3 (1978), pp. 221-5.

Snyder, B.R. *The Hidden Curriculum* (Massachusetts Institute of Technology Press, Knopf, New York, 1971).

Sofer, E.G. 'Inner Direction, Other Direction and Autonomy: A Study of College Students', in Lipset, S.M. and Lowenthal, L. (eds.) *Culture and Social Character* (Free Press, New York, 1961).

Solomon, L.C. 'Schooling and Subsequent Success', in Solomon, L.C. and Taubman, P.J. (eds.) *Does College Matter?* (Academic

Press, New York, 1973).
—— and Taubman, P.J. (eds.) *Does College Matter?* (Academic Press, New York, 1973).
Stern, G.G. *People in Context* (Wiley, New York, 1970).
Svensson, L. 'On Qualitative Differences in Learning: III — Study Skill and Learning', *British Journal of Educational Psychology*, vol. 47 (1977), pp. 233-43.
Thielens, W. (Jr) 'Undergraduate Definitions of Learning from Teachers', *Sociology of Education*, vol. 50 (1977), pp. 159-81.
Thoday, D. 'How Undergraduates Work', *University Quarterly*, vol. 11 (1957), pp. 172-81.
Thomas, L.F. and Harri-Augstein, E.S. 'Learning to Learn: The Personal Construction and Exchange of Meaning', in Howe, M.J.A. (ed.) *Adult Learning* (Wiley, London, 1977).
—— —— *The Art and Science of Getting a Degree* (Centre for Study of Human Learning, Brunel University, 1978).
Thomas, W.I. and Thomas, D.S. *The Child in America* (Knopf, New York, 1932).
Tinto, V. 'Dropout from Higher Education: A Theoretical Synthesis of Recent Research', *Review of Educational Research*, vol. 45 (1975), pp. 89-125.
Tomlinson, P. 'Some Perspectives from Academic Psychology', in Collier, G., Wilson, J. and Tomlinson, P. (eds.) *Values and Moral Development in Higher Education* (Croom Helm, London, 1974).
Trent, J.W. and Medsker, L.L. *Beyond High School* (Jossey-Bass, San Francisco, 1968).
Tricker, R.A.R. 'The Philosophical Context of Science Teaching: Theory as Dogma?' in *Aspects of Education*, no. 12 (University of Hull Institute of Education, 1971), pp. 102-9.
Turiel, E. 'Developmental Processes in the Child's Moral Thinking', in Mussen, P.H., Langer, J. and Covington, M. (eds.) *Trends and Issues in Developmental Psychology* (Holt, Rinehart and Winston, New York, 1969).
Vernon, P.E. *Intelligence and Cultural Environment* (Methuen, London, 1969).
Wallace, W.L. *Student Culture* (Aldine, Chicago, 1966).
Wankowski, J.A. *Temperament, Motivation and Academic Achievement*, 2 vols. (University of Birmingham, Educational Survey, 1973).
—— 'Counselling the Individual Student', in Hills, P.J. (ed.) *Study Courses and Counselling* (Research into Higher Education Mono-

graphs, Society for Research into Higher Education, Guildford, 1979).

Watts, A.G. *Diversity and Choice in Higher Education* (Routledge and Kegan Paul, London, 1972).

Watts, I. *The Improvement of the Mind* (Gale and Curtis, London, 1810).

Wells, S. 'Evaluation Criteria and the Effectiveness of Instructional Technology in Higher Education', *Higher Education*, vol. 5 (1976), pp. 253-75.

Whitehead, A.N. *The Aims of Education* (Benn, London, 1962).

Widick, C. and Simpson, D. 'Developmental Concepts in College Instruction', in Parker, C.A. (ed.) *Encouraging Development in College Students* (University of Minnesota Press, Minneapolis, 1978).

Wilkinson, A. *The Foundations of Language* (Oxford University Press, London, 1971).

Wilson, E.K. 'The Entering Student: Attributes and Agents of Change', in Newcomb, T.M. and Wilson, E.K. (eds.) *College Peer Groups* (Aldine, Chicago, 1966).

Wilson, J.D. 'Swots and Slackers: Students' Hours of Study', in *Students in Need* (Society for Research into Higher Education, Guildford, 1978a).

—— 'The Academic Achievement Game — Experience with Entering Students', *Scottish Educational Review*, vol. 10 (1978b), pp. 7-18.

Witkin, H.A. 'Psychological Differentiation', in Cashdan, A. and Whitehead, J. (eds.) *Personality, Growth and Learning* (Open University Press, London, 1971).

—— 'Cognitive Style in Academic Performance and in Teacher-Student Relations', in Messick, S. (ed.) *Individuality in Learning* (Jossey-Bass, San Francisco, 1976).

——, Goodenough, D.R. and Oltman, P.K. *Psychological Differentiation: Current Status* (Research Bulletin 77-17, Educational Testing Service, Princeton, New Jersey, 1977a).

—— *Field Dependence Revisted* (Research Bulletin 77-16, Educational Testing Service, Princeton, New Jersey, 1977b).

—— and co-workers, 'Role of the Field Dependent and Field Independent Cognitive Styles in Academic Evolution: A Longitudinal Study', *Journal of Educational Psychology*, vol. 69 (1977c), pp. 197-211.

—— and Goodenough, D.R. 'Field Dependence and Interpersonal

Behaviour', *Psychological Bulletin*, vol. 84 (1977d), pp. 661-89.
——, Moore, C.A., Goodenough, D.R. and Cox, P.W. 'Field Dependent and Field Independent Cognitive Styles and their Educational Implications', *Review of Educational Research*, vol. 47, no. 1 (1977e), pp. 1-64.

Woods, R.G. and Barrow, R. St C. *An Introduction to the Philosophy of Education* (Methuen, London, 1975).

Yeats, W.B. *Collected Poems* (Macmillan, London, 1955).

Young, M.F.D. *Knowledge and Control* (Collier Macmillan, London, 1971).

INDEX

ability 17, 34, 137, 150; spatial 133,
139; verbal 133
Academic Achievement Game 151-3
academic performance 17, 36, 43, 46,
51, 52, 69, 74, 90, 94, 95, 104, 140,
143, 151; cognitive style 135, 144-
5; prediction of 20, 153-7; study
methods and 100, 112-13; study of
150-3, 172
accommodation 26, 35, 36, 64
adaptation 17, 21, 26, 54, 111, 145,
168, 171
Adderley, K.A. 88
alienation 64, 72, 73
Allbrow, M.C. 94
Allport, G.W. 80
anxiety 17, 111, 115, 150
*Art and Science of Getting a Degree,
The* 117, 167-8
Asch, S.E. 146, 147
assessment 25, 56, 79, 96; diagnostic
75-6, 168-9; examinations 55, 81,
90, 100, 107, 111, 123, 130, 143,
169-70; methods 121-3, 169-72;
models 148-9; 'pass-fail' 54; staff
attitudes 44-5, 46, 75-6; student
perceptions 17, 48-53, 110-11; study
behaviour 110-11, 148-9
assimilation 26, 29, 35, 45, 54, 64
Astin, A.W. 19, 56-8, 59, 83, 89
atomist 106, 109, 112, 113, 116

Barnes, D. 171
Barrow, R. St C. 121, 128
Beach, L.R. 16
Beard, R.M. 16, 20, 44
Becher, R.A. 97, 170
Becker, H.S. 21, 33, 40, 44, 45, 47, 48,
50, 54, 94, 95, 143
Benington 59
Bernstein, B. 30
Biggs, J.B. 146, 148, 150, 161; presage,
process, product model 153-7
Black, H.D. 169
Bligh, D. 171
Blis, J. 148, 171
Bloom, B.S. 80, 116, 163
Bolton, C.D. 92, 93

Broadbent, D.E. 163
Brown, G. 16, 20, 76, 168
Bruner, J.S. 18, 25, 28, 115, 120, 123,
134, 137
bull 37-8, 73, 148
Burchill, J. 118

Cashdan, A. 123
Chibnall, B. 45
Chickering, A.W. 79
Clark, B.R. 52, 91
Cockburn, B. 168
cognitive approach 111, 113
cognitive skills 78
cognitive strategy 18, 111, 123
cognitive style 18, 135-49
Coleman, J.S. 91-3
college of education 41, 51, 95, 130
Collier, G. 55
commitment 66, 71-2, 84, 114, 165
concentrated study 88-9
Coombs, P.H. 99, 101, 102
counselling 75, 82; and mental health
35-6; and wastage 20, 36
cow 37-8, 148
Creedon, C.F. 90
Cronbach, L.J. 20
cue conscious 50
cue deaf 18, 50
cue seekers 18, 50, 53, 84, 145, 147,
151, 161
curriculum 18, 30, 51-3, 55, 79, 86-7,
144, 166; development of 169-72;
hidden 47-9, 116; informal 86

Dahlgren, L.O. 118, 168
Daniel, J.S. 128
Davie, G. 121, 171
décalage 20, 84
deficit model 62, 76, 82, 171
department characteristics 42-3, 51-3
depth processors 106-10
Desforges, C. 20, 76
Dewey, J. 25
Dimattia, P.A. 54
Dockrell, W.B. 169
Donaldson, M. 25, 26
Dressel, P.L. 42

DATE DUE

DEC 16 1998	
MAY 10 1999	

BRODART, INC.   Cat. No. 23-221